AGAINST ADIMANTUS,
DISCIPLE OF MANICHAEUS

St. Augustine
Bishop of Hippo Regius

Translated by: D.P. Curtin

Copyright @ 2021 Dalcassian Press

All rights reserved. No part of this publication may be reproduced, distributed, or transmitted in any form or by any means, including photocopying, recording, or other electronic or mechanical methods, without the prior written permission of the publisher, except in the case of brief quotations embodied in critical reviews and certain other non-commercial uses permitted by copyright law. For permission request, write to Dalcassian Press at dalcassianpublishing at gmail.com

ISBN: 979-8-3302-3443-1 (Paperback)

Library of Congress Control Number:
Author: Curtin, D.P. (1985-)

Printed by Ingram Content Group, 1 Ingram Blvd, La Vergne, Tennessee

First printing edition 2021.

AGAINST THE LOST DISCIPLE OF MANICHAEUS

1. 1. Concerning what is written: In the beginning God made the heavens and the earth; until that which is written: And it was done in the evening, and it was done in the morning one day. The most foolish Manichaeans think that this chapter of the Law is against the Gospel, saying that it is written in Genesis that God by himself made heaven and earth and light; and in the Gospel it is written that the world was made by our Lord Jesus Christ, where it is said: And the world was made by him, and the world knew him not. For they are rejected in three ways. First, because when it is said: In the beginning God made heaven and earth; The Christian accepts the Trinity itself, where not only the Father, but also the Son and the Holy Spirit are understood. For we believe not in three gods, but in one God, the Father and the Son and the Holy Spirit: although the Father is the Father, and the Son is the Son, and the Holy Spirit is the Holy Spirit. The unity of the Trinity is a long discussion in this place. Then, because where it is said: God said: Let it be, and it was done; there it is necessary to understand that he did what he did through the Word. But the Word of the Father is the Son. Therefore, this chapter of Genesis does not contradict, where it is written: And God said: Let it be, and it was done; in that place of the Gospel where it is said: And the world was made through him, that is, through our Lord; because he is the Word of the Father by whom all things were made. Finally, if therefore the Son is not understood in Genesis, because it is not said that God did things through the Son; nor in the Gospel through the Son does God feed the birds, and clothe the lilies, and the other innumerable things which the Lord himself says God makes the Father: although he does not say that he does them through the Son. And the testimony of the Apostles is also added, which he says of our Lord Jesus Christ: He is the firstborn of all creation; and by him all things were made in heaven and on earth, visible and invisible; and they say that this chapter is contrary to Genesis, where God is said to have made the world in such a way that the Son is not specifically named there: they are greatly mistaken; and they do not see, if this is so, that the Apostle himself is contrary to himself, when in another place he says one thing, from whom all things, through whom all things, in whom all things; and he

does not name the Son. But how this Son is not named, it is nevertheless understood; so also in Genesis: and how these two chapters of Paul do not contradict themselves; so neither is the Gospel of Genesis.

The Manichaeans, who oppose the New Testament, say that it is written in Genesis, that God rested on the seventh day.

2. 1. Concerning what is written: And on the sixth day God finished all his works which he had done, and on the seventh he rested from all the same works which he had done. At this point also the Manichaeans slander, and the opponents of the New Testament say that it is written in Genesis, that God rested on the seventh day from all his works which he had done: for the Lord says in the Gospel: My Father worketh even now. Which is in no way the opposite. For the Lord of the Jews rebuked the error of those who thought that God rested on the seventh day in such a way that nothing could be done on that day. And he rested from all his works which he had done, that he might no longer make the world with all that is in it: not, however, that he might also rest from the administration of the world. For it is not written: God rested from all his works, so that he would no longer work. But it is written: God rested from all his works which he had made: so that he was not then in the world of making, from which work he had ceased after the perfection; but he should work in administering, in which work the Lord intimated him to be. Nor does she rest, as if after labor God asked for a rest, but signifies that he ceased from the organization of natural things after the completion of those things, although he still works in managing them.

The Sabbath was not rejected but understood by Christians.

2. 2. But the observance of the Sabbath was not understood by the Jews, who thought that it was necessary to cease from those works which are effective for the salvation of men. Wherefore the Lord also brought them back in other places, with a wonderful comparison of the ox that fell into the well, and the cattle that must be loosed in order to be led to water. And the Sabbath, not repudiated, but understood by Christians, has indeed ceased to be observed

carnally, but is spiritually retained by the saints, who understand the voice of the Lord calling to rest, and saying: Come to me, you who labor, and I will restore you. Take my yoke upon you, and learn from me that I am gentle and lowly in heart, and you will find rest for your souls. For my yoke is easy, and my burden is light. This Sabbath, that is, this rest, is signified by the Scripture, which the Jews did not understand, and instead of the dispensation of the times they carnally followed the shadow, whose shadow as a body, that is, the truth, was to be given to us. But as that rest of God is insinuated after the manufactured world; so the rest which is promised to us, after the works which we have in this world, if they have been just, we shall obtain, that is to say, in the seventh and the same last part of the age, about which there is a long discussion. Therefore the Lord does not rescind the writing of the Old Testament, but forces it to be understood.

The Manichaeans say that this opinion is contrary to the New Testament, in which it is written that God formed a woman and joined her to a man.

3. 1. Concerning what is written in Genesis: And God said: It is not good to be only man; let us help him. And God caused Adah to sleep, and she fell asleep; and he took one of his ribs, from which he formed Eve, whom he brought to Adam; and he said: Therefore a man shall leave his father and mother, and shall cleave to his wife. In this place again the Manichaeans are slandered, saying that this sentence is contrary to the New Testament, in which it is written that God formed a woman and joined her to a man: therefore, because in the Gospel the Lord says: Everyone who leaves home, or wife, or parents, or brothers, or children for the sake of he will receive the kingdom of heaven a hundredfold in this time, and in the age to come he will inherit eternal life. In which slander I wonder that they are thus blinded, or rather I do not wonder: for their malice blinded them, as it is written. But still, who does not see in the New Testament so many precepts about loving a wife? For why do the opponents of this sentence of the Lord, in which he says that a wife should be left for the sake of the kingdom of heaven, say the Old Testament rather than the New Testament itself? That is wrong to say. For they are to be understood, not to be accused at random, which seem to the uninitiated to be contrary.

3. 2. For the Lord also being asked by the Jews whether it pleased him to let his wife go after a bill of divorcement had been given, he answered them saying: Have you not read that he who made them from the beginning made them male and female? and he said: For this reason shall a man leave his father and mother, and cleave to his wife, and the two shall be in one flesh? Therefore they are no longer two, but one flesh. Therefore, what God has joined together, let not man separate. They say to him: What, then, did Moses command to give a certificate of divorce and to let him go? Jesus says to them: Because Moses allowed you to put away your wives because of the hardness of your hearts; but from the beginning it was not so. But I say to you, whoever divorces his wife, except for the cause of fornication, causes her to commit adultery: and if he marries another, he commits adultery. Behold, they have the opinion of the Old Testament confirmed by the Lord himself against the incompetence of the Jews. At the same time he also testified to Moses that because of the hardness of their hearts he allowed them to be divorced. Do they even say that the Gospel is contrary to the Gospel? But if they say that this chapter is false, and that it was added by the corrupters of the Scriptures (for this is what they are wont to say when they cannot find what to answer); What if someone else says that it is presumptuous and false, which they themselves utter by saying to the Lord: Everyone who leaves home or wife or parents or children for the sake of the kingdom of heaven, etc.? The poor people do not understand how, when they say these things, they are trying to overthrow all the Christian faith. But the true faith and the discipline of the Catholic Church confirm that both are true and spoken by the Lord, and in no way are they contrary: because both the union of husband and wife is from the Lord, and the abandonment of the wife for the sake of the kingdom of heaven is from the Lord. For not because Jesus Christ raised the dead and gave them life, therefore life itself is not to be abandoned for the sake of the kingdom of heaven. Therefore, although the Lord has given a wife to a man, she must still be left, if need be, for the sake of the kingdom of heaven. For this is not always necessary, as the Apostle says: If a believer has an unbelieving wife, and she consents to live with him, let him not divorce her. It certainly means that if he does not agree to live with him, that is, if the faith of Christ is cursed in him, and he does not suffer him, because he is a Christian, he must be left for the sake of the kingdom of heaven, as the same Apostle says in what follows: If an unbeliever departs, let him depart; for a brother or a sister is not subject to such servitude. If, therefore, a man leaves the kingdom of heaven, while he does not want to leave a wife who does not bear a

Christian man, he is disapproved of by the Lord: and likewise if a man leaves his wife with a certificate of divorce, when there is no cause either of fornication or of obtaining the kingdom of heaven, he is likewise disapproved of by the Lord. Thus neither these two Gospel chapters are found to be contrary to themselves, nor the Gospel to the Old Testament: because there the wife is joined to the husband, so that together they deserve to inherit the kingdom of heaven; and so it is commanded that the wife should be left if she hinders the husband from inheriting the kingdom of heaven.

3. 3. And therefore when the apostle admonishes both Christians, that is, husbands and wives; Is it not so said: Love your wives, even as Christ also loved the Church and gave himself up for her? and: Let women be subject to their husbands as to the Lord; because the Church is also subject to Christ? Is not that which these wretches laugh at in the Old Testament, which is written: For this reason, a man shall leave his father and mother, and shall cleave to his wife, and the two shall be in one flesh? I mean in Christ and in the Church? Then he adds: Nevertheless, let every man love his wife as himself; but the woman should fear her husband. Does he not show in another place most clearly that the nature and union of both sexes consist of the Lord God, the creator and organizer, when he says: Nevertheless, neither woman without man, nor man without woman, in the Lord. For as the woman is from the man, so is the man through the woman: but all things from God? If these were willing to consider this, they would not, by separating some chapters and collating them against each other with great fraud, create darkness for the uninitiated; but they would feel that everything, both in the Old and in the New Testament, was written and confirmed by one Holy Spirit.

3. 4. For even in the Old Testament they have in Isaiah the prophet how many swords are promised: lest in the New earth they should think that they were praised by the Lord, where he says that there are some who have encamped themselves for the sake of the kingdom of heaven, and added: He who can take, let him take. For Isaiah also says thus: These things the Lord says to those with swords who keep my precepts and choose for themselves what I want and are capable of my testament. I will give them in my house and in my wall a most famous place, much better than sons and daughters: I will give them an eternal name, and it will never be lacking. For certain shadows and shapes of things

before the coming of the Lord, according to the wonderful and most orderly distribution of times, that people who received the Old Testament were held; yet in it there is so much preaching and foreshadowing of the New Testament, that no evangelical and apostolic discipline is to be found, however steep and divine precepts and promises, which even those old books lack. But the Holy Scriptures do not desire reckless and proud accusers, but careful and pious readers.

In the chapter of Genesis, in which Cain received the curse, that he might be punished by the barrenness of the earth, the Manichaeans slandering and desiring to show the contrary of the Gospel.

4. Regarding what is written in Genesis: And the Lord said to Cain: What have you done? The voice of your brother's blood cries out to me from the ground. Now you will be cursed from the face of the earth, which absorbed and received the blood of your brother from the slaughter of your hand: for you must work the ground, which will give you barren fruits. In this chapter of Genesis, in which Cain received the curse, that he might be punished by the barrenness of the earth, slandering the Manichaeans, and desiring to show the contrary of the Gospel, they seem to me to think that they were not dealing with men, but exactly as if they were cattle, who would hear them or read their writings; Thus they were abused by their inexperience and slowness of mind, or rather by their blindness of mind. Why did they say that this chapter is contrary to that in the Gospel, which the Lord says to his disciples: Do not think about tomorrow; for tomorrow he will think to himself. Look at the birds of the sky, for they do not sow, nor reap, nor gather into barns. It is as if Cain, the parricide, were to be compared to the disciples of Christ, so that since he deserved the punishment of the barrenness of the earth, it would follow that those who followed the Lord Jesus Christ and were preparing to preach the Gospel would suffer the same barrenness. Nay, even in these two chapters, of which they set the one of Genesis, the other of the Gospel, as hostile to them, so much friendship and concord is found, that nothing greater is to be desired. For what could be more appropriate, what could be more fitting than that barrenness should follow him, whose brother was killed by his crime, even as he labored in the land; but for those, through whose ministry in preaching the word of God, the brethren were delivered, even those who thought not at all of

the morrow should serve a fruitful land? But if in the Old Testament they are horrified by the curse of God that the earth has become barren to the sinner; why is it not in the New Testament that the cursed fig tree of our Lord Jesus Christ became dry, without any sin of its master? Likewise, if they are pleased with the Lord's sentence, with which he tells his disciples not to think about tomorrow, because God will take care of their food; why are they not also delighted with the prophetic sentence, with which he sang, saying: Cast your anxiety on the Lord, and he will feed you? So that in this way, if they can, the poor may understand that the things which are detested in the Old Testament about God are so true that they are also found in the New; and those things which they praise and preach in the New, are also to be found in the Old: whence the manifest concord of both Testaments becomes clear to those who understand well.

Man is made in the image of God, not only Genesis, but also the Apostle cries.

5. 1. Concerning what is written in Genesis: Let us make man in our image and likeness. This passage of the Manichaeans, where it is written in Genesis, that man was made in the image and likeness of God, they therefore say that it is contrary to the New Testament, because the Lord says to the Jews in the Gospel: You are of your father the devil, and you want to do the desires of your father: he was a murderer from in the beginning, and he did not stand in the truth, because the truth is not in him, and because in another place the Jews are called serpents, gentiles, and vipers. They do not understand that it was said of man before he sinned, that he was made in the image and likeness of God; but this is what is in the Gospel: You are of your father the devil, to be called sinners and unbelievers. For in the Holy Scriptures the name of sons is taken in three ways: one, according to nature, as Isaac the son of Abraham, or even the other Jews who come from the same origin; to another, according to the doctrine, that every one should be called his son in that matter, from whom he has learned something; as the apostle calls his children, who have learned the gospel from him; thirdly, according to imitation, as the apostle calls us children of Abraham, who imitate his faith. In two ways, then, the unbelieving Jewish sinners are called the sons of the devil by the Lord; or that they learned impiety from him, as the apostle says of the devil himself: Who now works among the children of unbelief; or that they imitate him, which is more relevant to what

was said about him: And he did not stand in the truth; because the Jews themselves did not stand in the truth of the law which was given to them, testifying to the Lord and saying: If you believed Moses, you would also believe me: for he wrote about me. According to the same sins, the poisons are also called the offspring of snakes and vipers.

5. 2. But not only Genesis, but also the Apostle cries out about man being made in the image of God, when he says: Indeed, a man should not cover his head, since he is the image and glory of God, but the woman is the glory of man. And in order that it may be plainly understood that man is made in the image of God, not according to the oldness of sin, which is corrupted, but according to the spiritual conformation, the same Apostle advises us to put off the habit of sins, that is, the old man, and put on the new life of Christ, whom he calls the new man. And to teach that we have lost this at some point, he calls it a renewal. For he says thus: Having put off the old man with his works, put on the new man, who is renewed in the knowledge of God, according to the image of him who created him. Sons of God, then, are men renewed in his image, and made like him to the point of loving our enemies: as the Lord says, we ought to love our enemies, that we may be like our Father who is in heaven. The Scripture teaches that it is placed in our power by God himself, when he says: He gave them power to become the children of God. But men are called children of the devil, when they imitate his impious pride, and fall from the light and height of wisdom, and do not believe the truth; such as the Lord argues when he says: You are of your father the devil, and the rest. In this place the evangelical prophet agrees, saying: I said: You are God's, and all the sons of the Most High; but you shall die as men, and fall as one of the princes.

And we must honor our parents, and yet we despise them with no impiety because of the announcement of the kingdom of God.

6. Regarding what is written in Exodus: Honor your father and your mother. Even to this place, where God commanded about honoring parents, that place of the Gospel is said by the Manichaeans to be contrary, where the Lord said to someone: I will go first to bury my father; He answered: Without the dead, let them bury their own dead; but you come and proclaim the kingdom of God.

Which is paid in the same way as that above, where it was said of the wife to be left: For the sake of the kingdom of heaven; because we must also honor our parents, and yet we despise them with no impiety because of the announcement of the kingdom of God. For if the Gospel is contrary to the Old Testament because of this opinion, it also begins to be contrary to the Apostle, who exhorts both children to honor their parents, and parents to love their children. And not only that, but also the Lord will be seen to be contrary to himself (which is wrong to believe), because in another place he says to the man who seeks eternal life: If you want to come to life, keep the commandments, in which he also mentions that: Honor your father and mother. By completing these commandments, he also grows to the love of God, in which is all perfection. For the love of one's neighbor is a certain step to the love of God. And therefore to the answer that he has kept all those commandments, he says that he lacks one thing, if he wishes to be perfect, to sell all that he has, and give to the poor, and to follow him. From which it is clear that the honor of the parents is to be preserved in their own degree, and yet in the comparison of divine love, especially if they are an obstacle, they ought not to be despised without any doubt. For you have also stated in the old Scriptures: He who says to his father or mother: I do not know you, and he who does not recognize his children, but he himself has known your testament. Therefore, if the love of parents is recommended in the New Testament, and the contempt of parents is recommended in the Old, the two Testaments agree with each other from each chapter.

By this agreement of the two Testaments it is sufficiently shown that God is not cruel, but that each one is cruel in himself by sinning.

7. 1. Regarding what is written in Exodus: I am a jealous God, giving to the children of the third and fourth generation the sins of the parents who hate me. To this place the Manichaeans say that that of the Gospel is contrary to what the Lord says: Be kind as your heavenly Father, who makes his sun to rise on the good and the bad, and the other thing which the same Lord says: Not only shall the brother who sins seven times be forgiven, but also seventy times seven. From whom, however, if I ask whether God does not punish his enemies, they will doubtless be troubled. For they say: God is preparing an eternal prison for the nation of darkness, which they say is hostile to God. And it is little, but they

do not hesitate to say that he will also punish his own members together with the nation itself. But when they come to the chapters of the Old and New Testaments, in order to deceive the ignorant, and accuse them of being contrary to them, they imagine themselves to be too good. But let them say to us, to whom the Lord will say: Go into the eternal fire, which has been prepared for the devil and his angels; if he spares all and condemns no one? Therefore it must be understood that it is right that God repays the sins of the parents to the children who hate him. For from what he added, those who hate me, it is understood that they are punished by the sins of their parents, who wanted to continue in the same perversity of their parents. For such are punished not by cruelty, but rather by the justice of God, and by their own iniquity, as the Prophet says: For the Holy Spirit of discipline will flee from falsehood and remove himself from thoughts that are without understanding, and will be rebuked by the coming iniquity, that is, a man will be rebuked by the iniquity that comes to him his own, when the Holy Ghost departed from him. And in another place: These things they thought, and erred; for their malice blinded them. And in another place: Each one is bound by the ropes of his sins. The apostle agrees with these testimonies of the Old Testament of the New Testament, saying: God gave them up to the lusts of their hearts. By this agreement of the two Testaments it is sufficiently shown that God is not cruel, but that each one is cruel in himself by sinning.

7. 2. Now that it is written in the third and fourth generation that vengeance should proceed, I think that nothing else is signified, except that from Abraham himself, who begins to be the father of the Jewish people, there are four ages since that which is now taking place, which Matthew the evangelist distinguishes. One is from Abraham to David: the other, from David to the migration into Babylonia: the third, from the migration into Babylonia until the coming of the Lord: thence to the end the fourth is assigned, as the old age of the age is longer than the other ages. We believe that these ages are set for generations, although each one consists of several generations. And since the third begins with the transmigration of Babylon, when the captivity of the Jews took place; but in the fourth, that is, after the advent of our Lord, the nation of Jews was completely uprooted from its own soil: this is to be understood by what has been said, that God will return the sins of the parents to the third and fourth generations, certainly lawfully and properly to those who continue to

hold the sins of their parents, as They chose to follow God's justice. For the prophet Ezekiel clearly shows that the sins of the father do not belong to the son who lives righteously.

7. 3. But what is said in the Gospel: Be kind as your heavenly Father, who makes his sun rise on the good and the bad; it is not contrary to the Old Testament. For God does this in order to invite you to repentance, as the Apostle says: Do you not know that the patience of God invites you to repentance? And yet for this reason it is to be believed that God will not punish those who, as the same apostle says, store up for themselves wrath in the day of wrath and revelation of the just judgment of God, who will render to each one according to his works. For this patience and goodness of God is also preached by the Prophet, saying: But you spare all, since all things are yours, you who love souls, and the innumerable others by which it is understood that both in goodness and in severity the mercy and justice of God's Testament are preached.

7. 4. But if they are moved by what has been said: I am zealous; Let them also be moved by what the Apostle Paul says: "The zeal of God is your zeal." For I betrothed you to one man to present a chaste virgin to Christ. For the Holy Scripture, speaking in our words, shows also by these words, that nothing worthy can be said of God. For why should not these words also be said of that majesty, of which whatever has been said is said unworthily? because all the wealth of all languages is preceded by an ineffable sublimity? For since husbands are wont to preserve the chastity of their wives with zeal, the power and discipline of God, by which he does not allow the soul to commit fornication with impunity, they called the zeal of the God of the Scriptures. But it is a fornication of the soul, an aversion from the fruitfulness of wisdom, and a conversion to the conception of temporal temptations and corruptions.

7. 5. But that which he says to the brother to be forgiven, not only seven times, but seventy times seven, he certainly says to the penitent. But God says to them that he will repay the sins of those who hate him, not those who are reconciled to him through repentance. For the Lord also says in the prophet: I do not want the death of a sinner so much that he returns and lives. From which it is

easy to see, both in that patience which invites to repentance, and in that indulgence which forgives those who repent, and in that justice which punishes those who refuse to be corrected, that both Testaments agree and agree with each other, as if both were written by one God.

The measure of vindication properly established by the carnal; but the remission of every kind of injury is not only precepted in the New Testament, but foretold long before in the Old.

8. Regarding what is written in Exodus: An eye for an eye, a tooth for a tooth; and so on. At this place of the Manichaeans, that in the old law equal vengeance is permitted, and it is said that an eye for an eye, and a tooth for a tooth must be destroyed, they slander in this way, as if the Lord himself had shown these two to him as opposed and opposite in the Gospel. For he himself says: You have heard that it was said to the ancients: An eye for an eye, and a tooth for a tooth; But I say to you, I will not resist; but if anyone strikes you on the cheek, give him the other also; and whosoever will contend with thee in judgment, and take away thy coat, let him also loose his mantle. In which two sentences the difference between the two Testaments is really shown, but still both established by one God. For since at first carnal men were burning to avenge themselves much more than was the injury of which they complained, the first degree of leniency was appointed for them, so that the measure of the injury received should in no way exceed the pain of the avenger. For in the same way he could sometimes give an injury to someone who had first learned not to overcome it. Whence the Lord, having already by the grace of the Gospel led the people to the highest peace, built another above this level; so that he who had already heard that he would not exact a greater revenge than anyone who had been injured, was pleased to give his whole self with a placated mind. Which also the Prophet preaches in those old books, saying: Lord my God, if I have done this, if there is iniquity in my hands, if I have returned evil to those who repay me. And another prophet says of this kind of man who endures injuries, and tolerates them very gently: He will give his cheek to the one who strikes him, he will be satisfied with insults. From this it is understood that the measure of exact revenge against the carnal, and the remission of every kind of injury, is not only a precept in the New Testament, but was foretold long before in the Old.

All the evidence from both Testaments about the visible God and about the invisible God are in harmony.

9. 1. Concerning what is written, that God spoke with Adam and Eve, and with the serpent, and with Cain, and with the rest of the ancients: among whom it is also written that he appeared to some, and that he was seen by them, not to one, but to many In the passages of the Scriptures, in which it is found that God spoke with men, and appeared to some: the Manichaeans are intrigued and say that everything is contrary to the New Testament, because the Lord says: No one has seen God at any time, except the only Son, who is in the bosom of the Father; he announced to us about it; and again what he says to the Jews: You have neither heard his voice at any time, nor seen his face, nor have his word abiding in you: because you have not believed him whom he sent. To them we answer by the same thing that is written in the Gospel: No one has ever seen God, except the only Son who is in the bosom of the Father; he announced to us about him, that the whole question could be solved: because the Son himself, who is the Word of God, not only in the last times, when he was deigned to appear in the flesh, but also before the constitution of the world, he announced about the Father to whom he willed, either by speaking or by appearing, either by some angelic power, or by any creature: because he is the truth in all things, and all things consist of him, and all things serve him at his command, and are subject to him; that he may also appear to the eyes through a visible creature to whom he wills, when he is pleased: when he himself, according to his divinity, and according to that which is the Word of the Father, coeternal with the Father, and unchangeable, by which all things were made, can only be seen by the most purified and most simple heart. And therefore in some places even the Scripture itself testifies that the angel was seen, where it says that God was seen. As in that struggle of Jacob, and he who appeared was called an angel. And when he appeared in the bush to Moses; and likewise in the desert, when he had already brought the people out of the land of Egypt, when he had received the law, God spoke to him. But whether in the bush, when he sent him; or afterwards, when he gave him the law, Stephen says in the Acts of the Apostles that an angel appeared to him. This is why we say that no one should think that the Word of God, by which all things were made, could be defined by places, and appear visibly to anyone, except through some visible creature. For just as the Word of God is in the prophet, and it is rightly

said: The prophet said, it is also rightly said: The Lord said; because the Word of God, which is Christ, speaks the truth in the prophet: so also he speaks in the angel, when the angel announces the truth; and it is rightly said: God said; and: God appeared; and again it is rightly said: The angel said, and: The angel appeared; when it is said from the person of the indwelling God, that from the person of the servant creature. From this rule also

The apostle said: Are you willing to accept the test of him who speaks in me of Christ?

9. 2. But if this moves, that in the Old Testament God also speaks to sinners, either to Adah or to Eve, or to the serpent; let them also pay attention in the New Testament to which the Lord set an example of a foolish and covetous man, how the Lord spoke to him when he said: Fool, this night let your soul be taken from you; whose will these things which you have prepared be? For when the truth is spoken even to sinners, it is spoken through every creature, and it is not spoken except by him who alone is true. But what he says to the Jews: You have not heard his voice at any time; therefore he says, because those with whom he spoke did not obey. He also says to them: Nor have you seen his face; because he cannot. But what he says: Neither do you have his word abiding in you; because in whom the word of God abides, Christ abides in him, whom they rejected. For when the Lord himself had said: Father, glorify me with that glory which I was with thee before the world was made; a voice sounded from heaven: And I glorified, and I will glorify. Which voice many of the Jews present heard, and yet they are not to be said to have heard it, because they did not obey in order to believe. Therefore, if it is not to be wondered at that the Word of God, that is, the only Son of God, who proclaims of the Father, to whom he wills by himself, to whom he wills through some creature is manifested either by sounding or by appearing, when yet he himself is seen by himself in the heart of the world, and through him the Father: For blessed are the pure in heart, because they themselves shall see God.

We refer the question to the Manichaeans, and what they brought forth of the New Testament, we bring forth of the Old Testament.

10. Concerning that which is written, which God spoke to Moses and said to him: Speak to the children of Israel: Take the first fruits of every man that you set aside for me, that is, gold, silver, brass, purple, fine linen, goat's hair, red skins of lambs, whole wood, oil for lighting, frankincense, precious stones, that is, beryls; and set up a tent in which I may dwell with you. The Manichaeans also raise the question here, and say that in the Gospel it is contrary to this place of the Scriptures, which says the Lord: You shall not swear, not even by heaven, because it is the seat of God; nor by the earth, because it is his footstool. For they dispute, and seem to say something great to themselves, when they say: How can that God, whose heaven is his seat, and whose earth is his footstool, dwells in a tabernacle made of gold, and silver, and brass, and purple, and the hair of cattle, and the skins was it built? Using also the witness of the apostle Paul, because he says that God dwells in unapproachable light. To whom we refer the question, and what they have brought forth of the New Testament, we bring forth of the Old Testament. For there it is found written before: Heaven is my seat, but the earth is my footstool: what house will you build for me, or what is the place of my rest? Has not my hand made all these things? Behold, the books of the Old Testament preach that God does not dwell in man-made temples: and yet the Son of our God, with a whip made of the remains, drove out of the temple those who sold oxen and doves, and overturned the tables of the money-changers; and he said: My Father's house shall be called the house of prayer, but you have made it a den of robbers. If any one, then, having been appointed to these two opposite chapters, wishes to deceive the ignorant, and to say that in the Old Testament God is magnified, whose seat is heaven, and earth his footstool, and it is denied that he dwells in a manufactured house; and in the New Testament his house is called a temple built by men: will not the Manichaeans admit, even late, that God's habitation, made by the hands of men, should be taken to have some meaning in both Testaments? and that God does not dwell in places made by men, is it preached in both Testaments?

We say that a zealous God and a just God are not opposites.

11. Concerning what is written in Exodus: Thou shalt not worship strange gods; and again: Your God is called zealous; for he was zealous. In this chapter it is written: Thou shalt not worship other gods. Nor is it surprising, since in their

sect they mention and recommend a very numerous family of gods: since they also came to those visible things, which they venerate and adore for the light of truth itself; and therefore displeases them what is written in Exodus: Thou shalt not worship strange gods. They also add that it was said for this reason: Your God is called zealous; for he who was zealous was zealous: that we may not love a God who is zealous, whose zeal we are not allowed to be jealous of other gods. And therefore they say that this is contrary to the Gospel, because the Lord says: Father is righteous, and the world has not known you; as if God cannot be said to be just, unless he allows us to worship other gods. For they assert that a just God and a zealous God are opposites to themselves, and deceive the poor, not understanding that the whole hope of our salvation is the zeal of God. For by this name of his is signified that providence, by which he permits no soul to commit fornication by himself with impunity, as the Prophet says: You will destroy all who commit fornication from you. For just as what is called the wrath of God is not a disturbance of the mind, but the power of revenge: so the zeal of God is not a torture of the mind, with which the husband is usually tortured against the wife, or the wife against the husband, but the calmest and most sincere justice, by which no soul is allowed to be blessed, by false opinions corrupted by evil desires, and in a way pregnant. For those who have not yet seen that no words match the ineffable majesty of God are appalled at these words. For in this way they think that they must be restrained from these words, as if they were saying something worthy of God, when they do not say these things. For the Holy Spirit, insinuating this very thing to men who understand, how ineffable the divine essence is, chose to use these words too, which among men are usually placed in vice; so that they may be reminded that even what men think they say with some dignity of God, is unworthy of his majesty, to whom silence is more honorable than any human voice. I search for the zeal of a man, and I find confusion that torments the heart. However, when I look for the reason, I find nothing else, except that the spouses do not tolerate adultery. For it is usually said that jealousy is especially common between married couples. Therefore, if the husband were blessed in himself and all-powerful and just, he would vindicate the sin of the spouse without any torture, and with all ease, and without any iniquity. However, his action in a human way of speaking, even if not literally, I would still translate and rightly call zeal. For who was slandered by Tullius, who certainly knew how to speak Latin, when he said to Caesar: There is none of your virtues, neither more admirable, nor more pleasing mercy? And yet they say that mercy is called from him, because the misery of others makes the heart of the afflicted miserable. Does virtue, then, make the heart miserable? What, then, would Tullius answer to the slanderers, except that he wished to call himself clemency by the name of mercy? For we are accustomed to speak correctly, using not only our own words, but also neighboring words. I wanted to mention the author, since the question here is not about the subject, but about the word. For just as our authors, that is to say of the divine Letters, thought most of all things; thus the worldly authors are almost entirely concerned with words. But I have the Gospel, and all the books of the New Testament, in which the mercy of God is most frequently commended. If, therefore, these poor people dare, let them also make a question from there, and deny that God is merciful, lest it should be understood that the poor have a heart. As, then, there can be mercy in God without misery of heart: so also without loss and torment of soul, we shall not be disdainful to receive God's zeal; and let us bring on the human condition of speech, that we may reach the divine silence. But if the opposites say that there is a zealous God, and a just God; what are they going to say, when I also find in the New Testament: God's zeal is your zeal; or a testimony also used of the ancients in the Gospel: Has the jealousy of your house eaten me up? Again in the Old Testament, when they read: The Lord is just, and he loved justices, he saw equity in his countenance; Will they not admit that even in this way the two Testaments may seem contrary to the uninformed, so that in the New we may find the zeal of God, in the Old the justice of God? but to those who understand well that both are reconciled in both the great unity and peace of the Holy Spirit?

From this it appears that flesh and blood will not inherit the kingdom of God, because when he has put on incorruption and immortality, he will no longer be flesh and blood, but will be changed into a heavenly body.

12. 1. Concerning what is written, that blood is not to be eaten, that the soul is the blood of the flesh. To this the opinion of the old Manichean Law from the Gospel opposes that which the Lord says, that those who can kill the body, but cannot harm the soul, are not to be feared; and they argue, saying: If blood is the soul, how can men not have power over it, when they do many things with blood, whether they receive it and set it up as food for dogs and fowls, or pour it out, or mix it with mud and mud? For these and innumerable other things

can be done without difficulty by men of blood. Therefore these insulting people ask how, if blood is the soul, the murderer of a man cannot harm the soul, since he has so much power over his blood. They also add what the Apostle Paul says: Because flesh and blood will not inherit the kingdom of God: and they say: If blood is the soul, as Moses says, no soul will be found able to obtain the kingdom of God. To whom the slander must first be answered in such a way that they themselves are forced to show where it is written in the books of the Old Law that the human soul is blood. For they will nowhere find this in that Scripture, which the wretches, as long as they try to tear, are in no way allowed to understand. But if nothing of the kind is said there about the human soul, what does it concern us if the soul of an animal can either be harmed by a murderer, or cannot inherit the kingdom of God? But because they are too concerned about the souls of cattle (for although the souls of men are rational, they still consider them turned into cattle), they think that the kingdoms of heaven are closed to them, if they agree that they are closed to the minds of cattle.

12. 2. What, that he even dared to insult the people of Israel, Adimantus, one of the disciples of Manichaeus, whom they mention to have been a great teacher of that sect? He therefore dared to insult the Jewish people, because according to their understanding, in which they think that the blood is the soul, the souls of their parents were partly devoured by serpents, partly consumed by fire, and partly withered in the deserts and most rugged places of the mountains. And if any one were to grant that it was true, he would be convinced that it had been done without the guilt of those whom he wished to insult. For they did not in some part injure the souls of their parents, to whom he said that all these things had happened according to their understanding: therefore they can have mourning from that, not guilt. But what will Adimantus himself do according to his opinion, in which even the rational believed, that is, that the souls of men can be built into beastly bodies? What, then, will he do about so great a crime, if he ever smote a sluggish beast, or tired out an excited bridle, in which perhaps his father's soul was? not to mention that he was also able to kill his parents among lice and fleas, from which they do not refrain from killing. For what does it profit them, that sometimes they deny that human souls can be turned down to the smallest of animals? For they deny this, lest they should be obliged to kill so many people, or be forced to spare lice, fleas, and bugs, and to endure

so much trouble from them without any permission to kill them. For they are vehemently urged why the human soul can turn into a fox, and not into a weasel; while the cub of a fox is perhaps even smaller than a large weasel. Then, if it can be a weasel, why can't it be a mouse? And if he can do this, why can't he do the stellion? And if it is possible for him, why is it not possible for the locust? Then to the bee, then to the fly, then to the bug, and from there to the flea, and if there is anything else much more minute, to arrive? For they do not find where they set the limit, and thus through this foolish credulity, their consciences are overwhelmed by the innumerable crimes of murder.

12. 3. For from what is written, that the blood of the cattle is its soul; apart from what I said above, it does not concern me what is said about the soul of the cattle; I can also interpret that commandment as being placed in a sign. For the Lord did not hesitate to say: This is my body; when he would give a sign of his body.

12. 4. But what the Apostle says: Flesh and blood shall not inherit the kingdom of God; It is also said in the Law: My spirit shall not abide in these, because they are flesh. And so often in the old books a future reward is promised to the souls of the righteous. However, the apostle wishing to insinuate what kind of body the righteous will be through change in the resurrection, because they do not marry, nor take wives, but they will be like the angels in the heavens. therefore, wishing to insinuate this future change of the bodies of the saints, the apostle said: For I say to you, brethren, that flesh and blood shall not inherit the kingdom of God. This can be found, not by a single isolated sentence, and fraudulently mentioned, but by perusing the entire passage of the Epistle, or rather by reading it (for it is not an obscure matter). For thus he says: It is necessary for this corruptible to put on incorruption, and for this mortal to put on immortality. What he says about the body is clearly found in the previous ones, when he says: All flesh is not the same flesh: some indeed of men, and some of cattle; some flesh of fowls, another of fish. And heavenly bodies, and earthly bodies: but the glory of the heavenly is one thing, and the glory of the earthly is another. another glory of the sun, another glory of the moon, and another glory of the stars. For star differs from star in glory; so also the resurrection of the dead. It is sown in corruption, it rises in incorruption: it is sown in reproach, it rises in glory: it is sown in weakness, it rises in strength: it is

sown in an animal body, it rises in a spiritual body. If the body is animal, it is also spiritual, as it is written: The first man Adam was made a living soul, the last Adam a life-giving spirit. But not first that which is spiritual, but that which is animal; afterwards, that which is spiritual. The first man from the earth, earthly; the second man from heaven, the heavenly Such as are earthly, such also are earthly; and the quality of the heavenly, such also the heavenly. And as we put on the image of the earthly, let us also put on the image of him who is from heaven. But I say this, brethren, because flesh and blood cannot inherit the kingdom of God; nor will corruption inherit incorruption. It is certainly now clear why the apostle said this. What, then, does he not mention in so base a fraud, except this last, and he is silent about those above, by whom this which he interprets wrongly can be well understood? For since the body of our Lord was so lifted up into heaven after the resurrection, that it received a heavenly change instead of the heavenly dwelling itself, and we are commanded to hope for this at the last day; therefore the apostle said: As earthly, such also earthly, that is, mortals; and such as are heavenly, such also are heavenly, that is, immortal, not only in souls, but also in bodies. Whence he had said above, that the glory of the heavenly bodies is one, and that of the terrestrial bodies is another. But what he said is that the spiritual body will be in the resurrection, we must not therefore think that it will be not a body, but a spirit: but he says that the spiritual body is in every way subject to the spirit, without any corruption or death. For it is not because what we have is called an animal body that it is not the body but the soul that is supposed to be. Therefore, just as the body is now called an animal, because it is subject to the soul; but it cannot yet be called spiritual, because it is not yet fully subject to the spirit, as long as it can be corrupted: thus and then it will be called spiritual, since it will not be able to resist any corruption to spirit and eternity.

12. 5. Or if still little seems to have been pointed out, that the apostle spoke this sentence because of the change which is to come, when he says: Flesh and blood cannot inherit the kingdom of God, nor will corruption inherit incorruption; pay attention to what he immediately submits and adds: Behold, I tell you a mystery: indeed we shall all rise again, yet we shall not all be changed, in an atom, in the twinkling of an eye, at the last trumpet. For the trumpet will sound, and the dead will rise incorruptible, and we will be changed. Then he closed it, and he also says what I mentioned a little before, in order to show

what the change itself will be. For he immediately says: For this corruptible must put on incorruption, and this mortal must put on immortality. From this, then, it appears that flesh and blood will not inherit the kingdom of God, because when he has put on incorruption and immortality, he will no longer be flesh and blood, but will be changed into a heavenly body. We have dealt with this from the occasion, because they are wont to make a great deal of noise about this point of view, denying the resurrection of the body. For this question is not proposed about the body, but about the soul, which they think is taken in this way in the Law, that it is considered to be blood: which we in no way understand in this way. But although we do not care about the souls of cattle, with whom we have no fellowship of reason, yet that which the Law said, that blood should be shed, and not taken into meat, because blood is the soul, we say to be set in a sign, like many other things; and almost all the sacraments of those Scriptures are full of signs and figures of the future preaching, which has already been declared by our Lord Jesus Christ. For the blood is thus the soul, just as Christ was the rock, as the apostle says: For they drank from the spiritual following the rock, but the rock was Christ. Now it is known that the children of Israel, struck by a rock, drank water in the wilderness, of whom the apostle spoke when he said these things; and yet he does not say: The rock signified Christ; but he said: The rock was Christ. Which, again, lest it should be taken carnally, he calls it spiritual; that is, he teaches it to be understood spiritually. It is long, and now not necessary, to explain the sacraments of the same Law, unless they can briefly. Now it is enough that those who are slandered about these should know that we do not understand them in such a way as they are wont to ridicule. but just as the apostles, understanding everything, expounded a few things, so as to leave the rest to posterity to understand the same rules.

We undertook to refute and refute the slanders of the diamond.

13. 1. Regarding what is written in Deuteronomy: See that you do not forget the testament of your God which he wrote, and make for yourselves images and images; He also added, saying: Your God is a consuming fire, and a jealous God. This is how Adimantus put forward these words from the Scriptures. For we undertook to refute and refute his slanders. But even above, when the jealousy of God was slandered, I think that the answer is sufficient. Let us remember,

however, not only there, but also here, that the Scriptures accused him of the jealousy of God, so that he may also add that the Lord our God commands in those books not to worship images; as if he did not blame the zeal of God for any other reason than that we are prevented from worshiping images by that very zeal: therefore he wants to be seen to favor images. This they do for this reason, so that their most wretched and vexed sect may win the favor of even the Pagans. And to this chapter of the Law they also oppose that, where a man came to the Lord and said to him: Good teacher, what shall I do to inherit eternal life? To whom Jesus answered: Why do you ask me about good? There is no one good but one God. So that we may decide from this that these are opposites, because in the Law it is said: God is a consuming fire, and: God is zealous; and in the Gospel: No one is good but one God.

13. 2. And concerning jealousy it has already been answered, that these words are not so placed in the Scriptures, as to signify some disturbance or torment of God; , they are forced to learn that even those things which appropriately think they speak of the ineffable divine excellence, are unworthy of the majesty of God; whose wisdom, when it had descended to the human body, first descended to human words. Behold, I said, come down: if I begin to discuss that word, I do not see that I have properly said it; for it cannot descend unless it can also be moved from place to place. For he who descends seems to leave a higher place and seek a lower one. But God's wisdom, since it is available in its entirety everywhere, cannot migrate from place to place under any circumstances. Of which John speaks better in the Gospel, as a partaker of the Lord's chest. For he said: He was in this world, and the world was made through him, and the world knew him not; and yet he adds and says: He came in his own, and his own did not receive him. How he was here, and how he came, except that that sublime ineffable, in order to suit men, must be signified by human sounds; but to make gods men, is the divine to be understood by silence? The reason can therefore be given why it was said so; yet nothing can be worthily said of God, which is therefore already unworthy, because it could be said. Take away error and pain from jealousy, what else will remain but the will guarding chastity, and vindicating conjugal corruption? By what word, then, but the jealousy of God, could it be better insinuated that we are called to the marriage of God, and does not want us to be corrupted by base love, and

punishes our immorality, and loves chastity? For it is not without reason that it is commonly said: He who does not zeal does not love.

13. 3. To this also belongs what was said: consuming fire; about which I must not argue, but rather ask them themselves, which fire the Lord said he came to send into this world. For this is said in the Gospel, that they cannot accuse them, not to honor Christ, but to deceive Christians. That was mentioned with them, as the Lord said: I have come to send fire into this world; the poor say: But that is another matter. To whom we answer: And this is another matter, do not be afraid. For Christ himself also speaks in the Old Testament, when he says: I am a consuming fire; who speaks in the Gospel that he came to send fire into this world, that is, the Word of God, which is himself. For indeed he expounded the old Scriptures to the disciples after the resurrection, beginning with Moses and all the Prophets, when the disciples themselves confessed that they had received fire, saying: Was not our heart burning within us on the way, when he opened the Scriptures to us? He is the consuming fire: for the divine love consumes the old life, and renews man: that from the fact that God is a consuming fire, he may cause us to love him; but from the fact that God is zealous, he will love us. Do not therefore fear the fire which is God's: but fear the fire which God has prepared for the heretics.

13. 4. For what Adimantus chose from the Gospel, which he would object to this chapter of the Law as contrary to the uninitiated, where the Lord says: No one is good but one God, whenever the goodness of God is found in the Old Testament, who is sufficient to count? However, I will add one thing, which is sung every day in the Church: Confess to the Lord, because he is good, because his mercy endures forever. Certainly this also seems to be the opposite of being zealous for God, as the Manichaeans think, and yet it is sung in the books of the Old Testament. Likewise, that king, who was about to make a wedding with his son, found among those reclining a man who had not a wedding garment; and calling him by the first name of his friend, ordered him to be sent with his hands and feet bound into the outer darkness. And if any one were to propose a chapter of the Gospel itself, and as Adamantus does of the Old Testament, so he would slanderously accuse the Gospel, instead praising the books of the Old Testament, where it is written: Give thanks to the Lord, for he is good, for his mercy endures forever; and criticizing in the New, that being called a guest, he

is sent to execution only because of his dress; and this he would constantly do with fraudulent perversity, so that he would gather all the places of gentleness from the Old Testament, and the places of severity from the New, and contend that these were contrary to him, praising the Old and criticizing the New: in the same way he would find the ignorant and miserably ignorant of the divine Scriptures, to whom the Old Testament would rather persuade , than to be retained as new. When they do this on the other side, that is, criticizing the Old as opposed to the New, I am surprised that they do not think that it is possible for someone to read both at some time, and with the help of God to praise the understanding of both; and their fraud and malice, either to be grieved as men, or to beware of them as heretics, or to be laughed at as ignorant and proud.

That all things should be clean and clean, kept under evangelical moderation.

14. 1. Concerning what is written in Deuteronomy: Kill according to the desire of your soul, and eat all flesh according to the pleasure which the Lord has given you. But be careful not to eat blood; but pour it out as water upon the earth. With these words, Adamantus thinks that the opposite of the Law is what the Lord says in the Gospel: Do not let your hearts be weighed down by crudeness, and wine, and worldly cares; and what the apostle says: It is good not to eat flesh, nor drink wine; and again: You cannot share the Lord's table with the table of demons. But we say that all these things, whether written in the Old Testament or in the New Testament, are placed in their exacting causes, and we show that they are not contrary to them. Although he himself was able to observe in these words which he put about the Old Testament, that what was said did not pertain to immoderate gluttony: Kill according to the desire of your soul, and eat all flesh; when it follows, according to the pleasure which the Lord has given you. For the Lord has not given you an immoderate pleasure, but such as is sufficient for the maintenance of nature and health. But whoever follows immoderate gluttony, follows his own vice, not the pleasure which the Lord has given: and therefore it is not contrary to what is laid down in the Gospel: Let not your hearts be weighed down by crudeness, and wine-indulgence, and worldly cares. For when every one is filled with nothing but that pleasure which the Lord has given, that is to say, modest and natural, his heart is not weighed down by crudeness, and wine-indulgence, and worldly cares.

14. 2. But concerning the not eating of meat and not drinking of wine, which the apostle says, not because he thought them unclean, he commanded this, as these men despise, and throw the erring into error, whom they have persuaded such things: but when he himself set forth the reason why he said this, it is not for us to interpret or explain this sentence. For it is sufficient to connect the whole passage of the Apostle's Epistle to this speech, so that the reason why the Apostle said this may be clearly seen. and the fraud of those who select certain parts from the Scriptures, by which they deceive the ignorant, not connecting what is written above and below, from which the will and intention of the writer can be understood. Thus the Apostle says: But receive the weak in faith, not in judgments of thought. Another, indeed, believes in eating everything: but he who is weak should eat vegetables. He who eats does not spurn him who does not eat; and he that eateth not, let him not judge him that eateth: for God hath received him. Who are you to judge a stranger's slave? He stands or falls to his master. But he will stand: for the Lord is able to establish him. One person judges alternate days, while another judges every day. Each one abounds in his own sense. He who knows the day, knows the Lord: and he who eats, eats the Lord; for he gives thanks to God: and he who does not eat, does not eat to the Lord, and gives thanks to God. For none of us lives to himself, and none dies to himself. For if we live, we live to the Lord; whether we die, we die to the Lord. Therefore, whether we live or die, we are the Lord's. For this Christ died and rose again, that he might rule over the dead and the living. But why do you judge your brother? or why do you reject your brother? For we shall all stand before the judgment seat of the Lord. For it is written: I live, says the Lord, because to me every knee will bow, and every tongue will confess to God. Therefore each of us will give an account for himself. Therefore, let us no longer judge one another: but judge this more, lest you cause a stumbling block or a stumbling block to the brethren. I know and am certain in the Lord Jesus, because through him nothing is common, except to him who thinks that something is common, to him it is common. For if your brother is grieved because of meat, you no longer walk according to charity. Do not lose him in your bait, for whom Christ died. Therefore our good will not be blasphemed. For the kingdom of God is not food and drink; but justice, and peace, and joy in the Holy Spirit. For he who serves Christ in this way pleases God and is approved by men. Therefore, let us pursue the things of peace, and the things of edification in one another. Do not destroy the work of God for the sake of meat. Everything is indeed clean, but it is bad for the person who eats through

offense. It is good not to eat flesh, nor to drink wine, nor in which your brother is offended. The faith that you have about yourself, have before God. Blessed is he who does not judge himself in what he tests. But he who discerns, if he eats, is condemned, because it is not from faith. But whatever is not of faith is sin. Does it need anyone's interpretation to understand why the apostle said this? and with what malice do they tear apart certain things from the Scriptures, with which they surround the ignorant? For the apostle also said that all things are clean according to faith; and that it is unclean for him who thinks it unclean: and then it is to be restrained from them, when they are taken by offense, that is, when a weak person thinks that he must be restrained from all meats, lest he should fall into the flesh of immolation; and therefore he who eats it may be thought to do so in honor of idols, and from this he is gravely offended: since the actual sacrifice of the flesh, if accepted by faith by the ignorant, defiles no one. Hence, in another place, the same Apostle forbids being asked, when something is bought from the butcher's shop, or when someone, being called by an unbeliever, sees meat being presented to him on his table, which they consider unclean, not because of sacrifice, but because they are meat. and that every creature of God is good, and that all things are sanctified by the word and prayer: and yet we must be moderated by them, if by any chance any weak person stumbles. And in a certain place he signified these very clearly, when he says, in the last times they will forbid certain people to marry, abstaining from the foods which God has created. For he specifically designates those who refrain from such foods, not because they either restrain their lust, or spare another's weakness, but because they think the meats themselves unclean, and deny that their creator is God. But let us hold to the apostolic discipline which says that all things should be clean and clean, kept under evangelical moderation, so that our hearts are not weighed down by rawness, and wine, and worldly cares.

14. 3. For the same thing which the Apostle says: You cannot share the table of the Lord with the table of demons; I do not see why this passage should be opposed to the Law, and as if they believed it to be the opposite of the Manichaeans. For the Law does not speak of sacrifices, when it is said in Deuteronomy: Kill according to the desire of your soul, and eat all flesh according to the pleasure which the Lord has given you; but about the foods that belong to the food of man. But since the Manichaeans also say that when

all animals are prepared for a man's meal, it is an immolation; according to their understanding they thought that these were opposites. For this reason they also mentioned that place where the Apostle says: Those who sacrifice to the Gentiles sacrifice to demons, and not to God; when the Apostle spoke most openly of the victims which are offered to demons in the temple; not of these foods which men prepare for themselves. For thus he says: What then? I say because something has been sacrificed to idols, or something is an idol? But because what they sacrifice, they sacrifice to demons, and not to God. I do not want you to become allies of demons. You cannot drink the cup of the Lord and the cup of demons. You cannot partake of the table of the Lord, and the table of demons. Do we emulate the Lord? Are we stronger than that? All things are lawful, but not all things expedient: all things are lawful, but not all things edify. Let no one seek what is his own, but what is another's. Eat everything that comes in the grocery store, asking nothing for conscience sake. For the earth is the Lord's and the fullness thereof. If someone from among the unbelievers calls you, and you decide to go; eat all that is set before you, judging nothing for the sake of conscience. But if anyone tells you that this is a sacrificial offering, do not eat it, for the sake of him who told you, and for the sake of conscience: and I mean conscience, not yours, but someone else's. Why is my freedom judged by another conscience? If I share with grace, even though I blaspheme, for what am I giving thanks? Therefore, whether you eat or drink, or whatever you do, do all to the glory of God. Let the Manichaeans pay attention to this, and let them see how it was said in Deuteronomy: Kill according to the desire of your soul, and eat all flesh according to the pleasure which the Lord has given you. For the fact that the Jews were commanded not to eat certain meats, and that they were said to be unclean, is valid for the meaning of the unclean people who are designated by figures in the old Scriptures. For just as that ox, whose mouth he forbids to be tied to the thresher, signifies the evangelist, as the apostle most openly explains; so also those things which are forbidden, signify certain human impurities, which are not received into the society of the body of Christ, that is, into the stable and everlasting Church. For as regards food, it is very evident that nothing is unclean at all, but that it is bad for the person who eats it through offense. Adamantus objected to the chapters of both Testaments as contrary and contrary to him.

15. 1. Concerning what is written in Leviticus: Separate the unclean from the world, and no one shall eat the flesh of a camel, donkey, hare, pig, eagle, kite, raven, vulture, or the rest. Nowhere can the soul of this man, most full of deceit and fraud, be detected, who objected to the chapters of both Testaments as being contrary and contrary to him, than in this passage where he mentions that it is written in Leviticus, that it should be tempered by some of the flesh of animals. For this sentence he believed to be opposed to that from the Gospel, where the Lord says: There is nothing that enters into a man and defiles him; but those things which proceed from him are confounded. If he did this imprudently, nothing more blind; but if knowingly, nothing more criminal. Had he not himself a little before borne witness to the Apostle, saying: It is good, brethren, not to eat flesh, nor to drink wine; while he wants from the New Testament of the Old adversary, where it is said: Kill according to the desire of your soul, and eat all flesh? How, then, does he like the sentence of the Lord, by which he says that there is nothing entering into a man that will defile him, but that which comes from a man will defile him? Where can he hide himself from this sentence? Where will he flee, he tells me, when he orders us to flee from the impurity of the flesh and to separate ourselves from the foods of the saints, with a perverted and superstitious imagination of continence? For certainly, if it is true, that the things which enter into man are not defiled, the Manichaeans, with great error, say that meat is unclean when men eat flesh. But if such meats are unclean, what will they do about this testimony, which was brought forth by evangelical and divine authority, where the Lord says that a man is not defiled by those things which enter into him, but by those which proceed from him? Or perhaps they are going to say, as they usually say, when the authority of the Scriptures urges them, that this chapter was inserted into the Gospel by the corrupters of the Scriptures? Why, then, does Adimantus use this chapter as a witness, and from there he tries to attack the Old Testament, from which it is prostrated? For when any Catholic Christian, venerable and understanding of both Scriptures, answered him, that these were not contrary; that those things concerning the flesh of certain animals, on which the still carnal people are commanded not to be eaten, are meant to signify human behavior, which the Church, which is the body of the Lord, cannot receive in its unity a stable and everlasting bond, as rejecting unclean meats, and in its not turning his bowels; so that all those precepts imposed on the carnal people prophesied the future spiritual discipline of the people: and therefore they are not contrary to the sentence of the Lord, by which he most truly says, that a

man should not be defiled by those things which enter into him through meat. For that sentence imposes burdens on servants; she now shakes off the yoke of slavery from her children. And yet it is said so, that the burdens of the slaves may foretell the faith of the free. For all things, as the apostle says, happened to them in a figure; but they were written for our sakes, on whom the end of the ages has come. If, therefore, they received into shape what they suffered, they received into shape what they were warned against.

15. 2. When, therefore, I have answered these things, and have shown that these two chapters of each Testament are not contrary in this way, what is he going to do, against whom he says the most weighty witness, which he himself produced against the adversary? For he himself mentioned the testimony of the Gospel, saying to the Lord that a man should not be defiled by those foods that enter into him: and he does not cease to advise and teach to abstain from meats as from unclean foods. And yet he felt how great a blow he had inflicted on himself, and how much he himself was wounded by the blow. For no one should question him and say: How then are you forbidden to eat meat, if the Lord says, as you yourself mention: There is nothing entering into a man, defiling him; but do those things which proceed from him coincide? He wanted to apply medicine without reason to a fatal wound. For in this way he set forth the gospel testimony itself. In the Gospel, he says, the Lord says to the crowd: Listen and understand: There is nothing entering into a man, defiling him, and so on. The fact that he mentioned that the Lord had said this to the crowd, shows nothing else, except that he did what he did out of ignorance, but malice: so that afterwards he would say to his hearers that the Lord had spoken to the crowd, and not to a few saints, such as they wish to think themselves; so that since they allow their hearers to eat meat as if they were still unclean, but think themselves to be wicked and evil when they are already clean, the Lord also seems to have felt this, because he did not teach these to a few saints, but to multitudes. O worst man, sure of the indifference of the human race to conceal its deceptions! For he did not believe that there was anyone who would take the Gospel, and read it with knowledge, and find a man in the very meadows where the Lord feeds his flocks, hiding snares for the unwary and less well-prepared. For the disciples were moved by these words, and did not believe that the Lord had spoken literally, but rather figuratively, when he said that a man should not be defiled by those things which enter into him through food, since the

disciples themselves were also Jews, who, fleeing from certain types of meat, had taken the food prescribed from childhood, approaching They said to him: Do you know that the Pharisees were offended when they heard the word? But he answered and said: Every plantation which my heavenly Father has not planted will be uprooted. Allow them; they are blind, and leaders of the blind. But if the blind leads the blind, they both fall into the pit. When, then, he called the unbelief of the Jews a planting which the heavenly Father had not planted, Peter still thought that it was a parable, and therefore reproached the Jews and the blind, saying that they could not understand it, answering said to him: Let us eat this parable. And he, clearly showing that it was not a parable, but a proper expression, said to them: Are you still without understanding? Don't you understand that everything that enters the mouth goes into the stomach and is expelled? But the things that proceed from the mouth proceed from the heart, and they defile a man. For from the heart proceed evil thoughts, murders, adulteries, fornications, thefts, false testimonies, blasphemies; these are the things that defile a man. But eating with unwashed hands does not defile a person. Now the Jews had raised a question about unwashed hands, on which occasion the Lord spoke generally about things that enter the mouth, and go into the stomach, and are sent into retirement, that is, about our food. Although it is written that when the multitudes were gathered to him, he said: It is not what goes into the mouth that defiles a man, but what comes out of the mouth; yet the fear with which he added this to his words, to which he mentioned this kind of testimony, is sufficiently evident, as was said a little before, that he had something to answer those who raised the question to him, why the chieftains of the Manichaeans think that it is wrong for them to eat meat: namely, that which the Lord says, It would seem that he had conceded only to the multitudes, not to the elect. But when it was made clear from the consequences that even Peter, who was questioned separately, and the listening disciples, whom he was certainly bringing to the summit of the Church, answered the Lord in such a way that he did not testify that he had said it through a parable, and showed that it belonged to all; they have no place to take food from the mouths of men, and fasten them with the snare of superstition.

15. 3. Perhaps one of them will say: What then does eating signify the flesh of swine, and camels, and hares, and kites, and ravens, and the rest, from which it is commanded in the Law to abstain? I don't want to, because it's too long. But

make sure I can't; Is that why no one can? And there are now innumerable volumes in which these things are set forth. It is sufficient for us to rebuke these, that these observations are a shadow of things to come, not I, but the Apostle says, when he also forbids them to be observed servilely, but nevertheless declares that they mean something, saying: Let no one judge you therefore in food, or in drink, or in part of the feast day, or of the New Year, or of the Sabbath, which is a shadow of things to come. Those futures, therefore, which were signified by those observations, after they came through the Lord Jesus Christ, the servile observations were taken away: but their interpretations are held by the children. For whatever signified the future Church is a prophecy. But you have the same Apostle saying: Do not reject the Spirit, do not extinguish prophecy; read all that is good; The legend is therefore divine Scripture, and the dispensation of the Holy Spirit to be known, and prophecy to be observed; and carnal servitude to be rejected, and liberal understanding to be retained.

The Lord confirms the authority of the Law, and yet he clearly shows that the behavior of those who did not obey the Law is to be avoided and avoided.

16. 1. Regarding what is written in Deuteronomy: Observe and sanctify the day which the Lord commanded you. Six days you shall labor and do all your work; but on the seventh day of the Sabbath you shall feast to the Lord your God, doing no work yourself, or your son, or your daughter, or your boy, or your girl, your ox, or your ass, all your cattle, or your tenant. And so shall thy servant and thy handmaid rest, even as thou also. Remember that you were a slave in Egypt, and the Lord your God redeemed you with a mighty hand and a high arm. Therefore the Lord commanded you to keep the seventh day. And again in Genesis it is written how Abraham speaks of circumcision: Keep my covenant, he says, you and your seed that will be after you. This is my covenant which you shall keep between me and you and your seed: you shall circumcise every male in the flesh of their foreskin; and let this be the sign of the covenant between me and you. And on the eighth day you shall circumcise all the males in your nation, so that you may also circumcise the master and the subject, except the foreigner: and this shall be a testament in your nation. And every male who does not circumcise his foreskin will lose his life from among the people, because he breaks my covenant. Adamantus sets forth all these words of

the Old Testament to be opposed to them of the New Testament, and affirms that they are contrary to what the Lord says in the Gospel about proselytes: Woe to you, hypocritical scribes and Pharisees, who go about sea and land to make one proselyte; and when you do, he will be a son of hell, much more than you are. As if for this reason the Lord calls a proselyte a son of hell, because he is circumcised and observes the Sabbath; and not rather because he is compelled to imitate the lost manners of the Jews and their perverse conduct, not by which they observe the precepts of the Law, but by that which they do contrary to the Law. In another place he says very openly about these, where he says that they reject the commandment of God in order to confirm their constitution: because when the Law commanded that father and mother should be honored, they themselves instituted how parents should be dishonored. And again with them he says: Woe to you, scribes and Pharisees, who have the key to the kingdom of heaven, you do not enter yourselves, nor do you allow others to enter. Or in another place he commanded his hearers to obey the sayings of the Pharisees and Scribes, but not to imitate their deeds. For he said: They sit upon the seat of Moses: do what they say; but do not do what they do: for they say and do not do. In which place the Lord confirms the authority of the Law which was given through Moses, and yet He clearly shows that the behavior of those who did not obey the Law which they had received should be avoided and avoided. And by these perversions of theirs they did, so that when a Gentile passed over to their Law, that is, he became a proselyte, had their manners, and became a son of hell, much more than they were themselves. For they took great pains to make one of the Gentiles a Jew, and forced the Jew who had become a Jew to imitate their worst manners.

It is not a shadow to be shaped in the body, but the very thing to be carried in the heart.

16. 2. Nor could Adamantus the Manichean point out that what he mentions about the Apostle as contrary, was not contrary at all; because his whole eye was not directed to the investigation, but to the criticism of the Scriptures. For he mentions the Apostle saying: Is anyone called circumcised? do not bring the foreskin. Who was called in the foreskin? he must not be circumcised: because foreskin is nothing, and circumcision is nothing, but the observance of the precepts of God. For what can be more manifest than this commanding of the

Apostle, that every one should remain as he was called? For the coming things of which those shadows were observations, this act was done, in order to show that hope was not to be placed in the shadows themselves, but in the very things which those shadows signified were to come, that is, Christ and the Church. And therefore all these things were already empty: yet the Apostle commands them not to be removed as harmful, but as superfluous, to be despised; so that if any Jew had believed in Christ, because of the offense of his own people, he would not be prevented from remaining in the superfluities themselves, and yet would not think that his salvation was established in them; And therefore circumcision is nothing, and circumcision is nothing, but the observance of the commandments of God. And what he says in another place: Would that those who trouble you would be cut off; not because circumcision is contrary to the Gospel, says the Apostle, as the Manichaeans think: but it is contrary to the Gospel, so that everyone who forsakes the thing which is represented by that shadow, follows the emptiness of the shadow itself. What they wanted was those who imposed the yoke of circumcision upon the Gentiles who believed in Christ, as if it were necessary for salvation, since it was no longer a shadow to be shaped in the body, but the very thing to be borne in the heart.

We prove the difference between the two Testaments in this way, that in the one there are the burdens of the slaves, in the other the glory of the free.

16. 3. And what he says: Observed days, and sabbaths, and solemnities; I fear you, lest I should have labored in you in vain; it is not written as Adimantus puts it. For the apostle does not mention the Sabbath there. For he says: You observed days and years and seasons; I fear you, lest I should have labored in you in vain. But suppose that it was said about the Sabbath. Do we not also say that these are not to be observed, but rather those which are signified by these? For they slavishly observed them, not understanding to what significance and prediction they pertained. The apostle blames this in them, and in all who serve creatures rather than the Creator. For we also solemnly celebrate Sunday and Easter, and any other Christian festivals of the day. But because we understand to what they belong, we do not observe the times, but what is signified by them by the times. But the Manichaeans criticize them in this way, as if they observed no days and seasons. But when they are questioned about these things

according to the opinion of their sect, they try to explain everything, so that they seem to observe not the times themselves, but the things of which they are signs. It is shown in other places that these things are legendary and most false. Now it was said to this, that they might be compelled to confess with their own mouths, that such things could reasonably be celebrated: and therefore it is manifest that the circumcision of the flesh was rightly imposed upon servants, and rightly understood by children. Let us therefore reject the carnal with the Apostle, and approve the spiritual with the Apostle: and we do not observe the rest of the Sabbath in season; but we understand the temporal sign, and to the eternal rest, which is signified by that sign, we direct the line of our mind. Let us, therefore, reject the observance of times with the Apostle, and let us hold the understanding of temporal signs with the Apostle: we prove the difference of the two Testaments in this way, that in the one there are the burdens of slaves, in this the glory of the free; in that the foreshadowing of our possession should be known, in that the possession itself should be held. The Apostle interprets the Sabbath to the Hebrews, when he says: Let Sabbathism therefore remain for the people of God. Circumcision is also interpreted when he says of Abraham: And he received the sign of circumcision, the seal of the righteousness of faith. Therefore I hold to the apostolic interpretation spiritually: I despise the carnal observance of servitude for freedom, honoring the God who is the author of both Testaments, who opposed the old fleeing man as a master that he feared, and opened to the new returning as a father that he would love.

We say that what was said to that people about killing their enemies is not contrary to the evangelical commandment about loving their enemies.

17. 1. Concerning what is written in Exodus: If you will hear my voice with your ear, and do all that I command you; I hate those who hate you; and I will grieve those who grieve you. and you shall kill them. You shall not worship their gods, nor do their works; but overthrow them by overthrow, and blot out their memory. With these words of the old books thus mentioned, Adamantus contradicts what is written in the Gospel, saying to the Lord: But I say to you: Love your enemies, bless those who curse you, and do good to those who hate you, and pray for those who persecute you . In this place it must first be seen that it should have been sufficient for the man who wanted to point out the

contrary, that it was written about the killing of enemies in the old Law. For the Lord, of course, commanded men to love their enemies; which through our patience and charity can be converted to salvation, and everyone understands, and it has been demonstrated very often by examples. What, then, does he mean by the fact that he thought that the consequences should be added, where it is written: Ye shall not worship their gods, nor do their works; but overthrow them by overthrow, and blot out their memory; but because they force the Manicheans to love the gods of the Gentiles? And what the Lord says in the Gospel: Love your enemies, they are thought to belong not only to men, but also to demons, or even to idols. But if it is so, who would not detest this madness? But if they do not think this, he greatly erred, who wanted to mention the precepts in the Old Testament that the superstitions of the Gentiles should be overthrown, while in the New Testament what is written about loving one's enemies, as if he wanted to oppose the opposite.

17. 2. But we do not say that what was said to that people in the old books about killing their enemies is contrary to this evangelical precept, by which the Lord commands us to love our enemies: since that killing of enemies was still in accordance with the carnal people, to whom the Law was given as a teacher it was, as the apostle says. As for those who at that time were very few holy and spiritual men in that people, like Moses, like the Prophets, with what intention they carried out that slaughter of their enemies, and whether they loved those whom they were killing, much is hidden from the uneducated and impious, who love their blindness. who, since they are not qualified to see these things, are rather to be pressed by the bulk of authority. For what is it that the apostle says: I, indeed, being absent in body, but present in spirit, have already judged as present him who has thus worked, in the name of our Lord Jesus Christ gathered together with you and my spirit, with the power of the Lord Jesus, to deliver such Satan to the destruction of the flesh. that the spirit may be saved in the day of the Lord Jesus? For what does that slaughter have, which these people exaggerate so much and fan with envy, but the destruction of the flesh? But since the apostle had explained with what intention he was doing it, he made it sufficiently clear that vengeance on any enemy could be proceeded with charity. And yet here also perhaps the destruction of the flesh, which takes place through repentance, can be understood in another way. But they read the apocryphal writings, which they also say are most incorruptible, where it is

written that the apostle Thomas cursed a man whom he inadvertently struck with a palm, not knowing who he was, and that curse immediately came to fruition. For when that man, being the minister of the banquet, had gone out to fetch water, he was killed and torn to pieces by a lion. To make it manifest to the terror of others, the dog brought his hand to the month where the apostle was convivial; and hence the beginning of the commendation of the Gospel. If someone wanted to turn the teeth of the Manichaeans against them, how bitingly he would criticize them! But since even there it is not silent in what spirit it was done, it seems the love of the avenger. Thus indeed it is read in that scripture, that the apostle interceded on behalf of him against whom vindication was temporally vindicated, that he might be spared in the future judgment. If, therefore, at the time of the New Testament, when charity is especially recommended, fear was injected into the carnal from divinely visible punishments; how much more is it to be understood that in the time of the Old Testament this suited that people, who were controlled by the fear of the Law as a teacher? For this is the briefest and most open difference between the two Testaments, fear and love: the former pertains to the old, the latter to the new man; yet both were brought forth and united by the most merciful dispensation of one God. And in the old Scripture the mind of the avengers is silent, because very few spiritual ones knew what to do with divine revelations, so that the people to whom terror was useful should be subdued by the most severe rule: so that just as they saw that they were given into their hands to kill their wicked enemies and worshipers of idols, so they themselves feared to be given into the hands of their enemies. , if they despised God's commandments of truth, and slipped into the worship of idols and the impieties of the Gentiles. For even those who sin in the same way are not differently vindicated. But all this temporal vengeance terrifies weak minds, that it may educate those who are nourished under discipline, and turn them away from everlasting and ineffable punishments: for carnal men fear more what God vindicates in the present, than what threatens the future.

17. 3. Therefore there can be love in the avenger. What every one tries in his son, when he falls into the worst manners, he constrains him with the most severe restraint, and all the more, the more he loves him, and thinks that in this way he can be corrected. But they do not kill the children whom men love when they want to correct them: because many consider this life a great good,

and the whole reason why they want to educate their children is that they hope in this life. But faithful and wise men, who believe that there is another better life, and know in part what they can do; nor do they themselves take revenge by killing, when they want to correct their children, because they believe that they can be corrected in this life. not because he hates them in so far as they are men, but in so far as they are sinners. For in the very old books we read that it was said to God: And you did not hate anything that you did; but all things, whether by means of punishments or by means of rewards, are regulated by justice. Was not the Apostle Paul speaking to the faithful Christians when he said: "But a man proves himself, and thus eats of the bread and drinks of the cup." For he who eats and drinks unworthily eats and drinks judgment for himself, not judging the Lord's body. Therefore there are many among you who are weak and sick, and they sleep enough. But if we were to judge ourselves, we would certainly not be judged. And while we are judged, are we rebuked by the Lord, lest we be damned with the world? Behold, it is manifest that God corrects with love, not only with infirmities and illnesses, but also with temporal deaths, those whom He does not want to condemn with the world.

17. 4. Let these men attend to these things, and let them see how the wicked nations could also be given into the hands of the people, though still carnal, yet worshiping one God, so that they might be killed by him; whereas among that people, if they were spiritual, they would understand the dispensation of God without hating anyone. the interjections of the widow's woman asking him to vindicate himself, though he was unjust, neither fearing God, nor reverent of men, yet he could not endure, and he listened to her, lest he should suffer further vexation: in comparison of which he said much more to God, who is most kind and just, to vindicate the elect their own from their enemies. Let these dare to put a question to him, and say, if they can: What is it that you commanded us to love our enemies, and you intend to avenge us of them? Or perhaps he is going to act against the will of his saints, by punishing and condemning those whom they love? Rather, let them themselves be turned from this slanderous blindness to God, and understand his will in both Testaments, lest they be found on the left side among those to whom the Lord is about to say: Go into the eternal fire, which is prepared for the devil and his angels. For I was hungry and you did not give me anything to eat; and so on.

For it is displeasing to these wretches that God has given his enemies over to his people to kill them; and they themselves forbid bread to be given to the beggar, not to the enemy, but to the executed. Rather, they understand that revenge can exist without hatred, which few understand: and yet as long as it is not understood, so long is it necessary for the reader to be tossed about in the books of both Testaments with great effort or error, and thinks that the Scriptures are contrary to him.

17. 5. What revenge the apostles had not yet taken in their hearts without hatred, when, angry with those from whom they had not received hospitality, they inquired of the Lord whether he wished them to ask fire from heaven, as Elijah had done, with which fire inhospitable men were consumed. Then the Lord answered them, saying that they did not know whose spirit their children were, and that he himself had come to deliver them, not to destroy them, because they, in an enemy's spirit, desired to destroy those whom they wished to be consumed by fire. Later, however, when they were filled with the Holy Spirit and became perfect, who could now love even their enemies, they received the power to avenge, because they could now avenge without hatred. What power did the Apostle Peter use in that book, which these do not accept, because it clearly contains the coming of the Paraclete, that is, the comforter of the Holy Spirit, whom he sent to the mourners, when he himself had ascended from their eyes into heaven. For the Comforter is sent to the sorrowful, according to that sentence of the same Lord: Blessed are they that mourn, for they themselves shall be comforted. He also says: Then the children of the bridegroom will mourn, when the bridegroom has been taken away from them. In that book, then, where it is most openly declared that the Holy Spirit, whom the Lord had promised to be the Comforter, had come, we read that men fell to Peter's opinion, and that the man and wife who had dared to lie to the Holy Spirit were dead. That they reproached with great blindness, when they read in the apocrypha as great, and that which I mentioned about the apostle Thomas, and that Peter's own daughter became paralyzed at the prayers of her father, and that the gardener's daughter died at the prayers of Peter himself; and they answer that this was expedient for them, that she might be relieved of her paralysis, and that she might die: yet they do not deny that it was done at the prayers of the Apostle. But who said to them: It was not expedient to slay the wicked nations, who mockingly pretend to be surprised that they were handed

over from God into the hands of the Jewish people? But since the Apostles did these things not with hatred, but with a good heart; whence do these convince the minds of the spiritual men who were among that people, that they hated them, who through them were commanded by divine justice to be removed from this life? Rather, let them check their rashness and not deceive the uninformed, who either do not have time to read, or do not want to read, or read with a perverted mind; and they do not pay attention to the fact that both the mercy and the severity of God are commended in the letters of both Testaments. For concerning the love of the enemy, that evil may not be returned for evil, we read in the old books: Lord my God, if I have done this, if there is iniquity in my hands. If I have repaid those who repaid me wrongs, let me fall with merit from my enemies in vain. Who would say this, unless he knew that this pleased God, so that no one would return evil for evil? But this is of the perfect, that they hate nothing but sins in sinners, but love men themselves; and when they avenge, they avenge not with the bitterness of cruelty, but with the moderation of justice; lest the remission of sin should be more injurious to the sinner than the punishment of vengeance. Nor yet did righteous men do this, except by divine authority; Let no one think that he is permitted to kill whomever he pleases, or to persecute by judgment, or to afflict with any punishments. Sometimes, however, the divine authority itself is clearly stated in the Scriptures, but sometimes it is hidden, so that the reader may be instructed in the obvious, and trained in the obscure.

17. 6. Certainly David took into power his enemy and persecutor, King Saul, who was very ungrateful and very hostile, so that he could do to him what he wanted; and he chose to spare rather than to kill. For he was not commanded to kill, but neither was he forbidden: nay, he had also heard from God that he could do whatever he pleased to the enemy with impunity; and yet he contributed so much power to meekness. Let me be told whom he feared, when he would not kill. Nor can we say that he feared the man whom he had taken into power; nor God, who had given Where, then, there was neither difficulty in killing, nor fear, love spared the enemy. Behold, that warrior David fulfilled Christ's commandment, which we received, to love our enemies. And would that they would imitate this, who have twisted the human feeling of compassion into some cruel delirium! For as long as they believe that the bread is crying, which cannot be done, they do not give it to the person whom they

see crying. Perhaps they will say, as the blind are wont to hurl mad insults, that David who spared the enemy was better than God who gave him the power to kill: as if indeed God did not know to whom he gave this power. He certainly knew the will of his servant, but in order that the other men also might learn to imitate that which in David's heart was already known to God as the love of the enemy, he gave him power over an enemy whom he did not yet want to be killed, because of the certain dispensation of things which had to be fulfilled through him. Thus David's goodness was commended, that men might have what they loved; and the wickedness of King Saul was extended to a more worthy end, that men might have something to fear.

That temporal goods are despised is shown in the books of the New and Old Testament.

18. 1. About what is written in Deuteronomy: If you hear the voice of the Lord your God with your ear, blessed are you in your field, blessed are you in your meadow, blessed is the fruit of your belly, and the fruit of your land, and the generations of your cattle, and your herd of cattle of yours, and your flock of sheep; You are blessed in your entrance and exit. They say that in the Gospel it is contrary to this chapter: If any man will come after me, he must deny himself, and take up his cross, and follow me. For what does it profit a man if he gains the whole world, but suffers the loss of his own soul? Or what shall a man give in exchange for his soul? But from that rule it is shown that there is no contrary, by which it should be known by now, that carnal and temporal rewards were promised to the carnal people in accordance with the same, but still by one God, whose creation is all, both superior and inferior. For certainly Adimantus himself gave testimony of the Gospel, where the Lord says: Do not swear, not even by heaven, because it is his throne; nor by the earth, because it is his footstool. And it is written in the old books: Heaven is my throne, and earth is my footstool. What wonder, then, if he gives the goods of his throne to those who serve him spiritually, and the goods of his footstool to those who serve him carnally? when the spirit is superior, and the flesh inferior, just as the heavenly are superior and the terrestrial inferior? Although all these, that is, the field, and the meadow, and the fruit of the belly, and the fruit of the earth, and the cattle, and the herd of oxen, and the flock of sheep, can also be understood spiritually. But now that discussion does not belong to the matter. But if in the New

Testament itself, whose reward and inheritance belongs to the new man, yet the Lord also promises to those whom he wants to be despisers of temporal things, to serve him in the Gospel, the multiplication of the same things in this world, saying that they will receive only a hundredfold in this world , but in the world to come I shall have eternal life; as it is also said in the old Scripture: To a faithful man the whole world is riches. Wherefore the apostle exults, saying: As if they had nothing, and possessed all things; If, therefore, in the New Testament, in addition to the eternal possession which is promised to the saints, the multiplication of this possession, which is to pass away, is not withdrawn, and it becomes so much richer, the more despised it is possessed; how much more in the Old Testament should the rewards of the carnal people have been such, yet by the one and true God, the ruler of all times, controlling and administering all things for the time.

18. 2. But lest in the books of the New Testament alone these things should be thought to be despised, let them hear the prophet rejecting such happiness, and singing that one should take refuge in the Lord God. For thus he says: Deliver me from the evil sword, and deliver me from the hand of the sons of strangers, whose mouth has spoken vanity, and their right hand the right hand of iniquity. Whose own children are like young women established in their youth. Their daughters were composed and adorned like the likeness of a temple. Their cellars were full, belching from one thing to another. Their sheep are fruitful, multiplying in their exits; their cattle are fat. There is no fall of the fence, no exit, no cry in their streets. They said blessed are the people to whom these things are; blessed is the people whose Lord is their God. Let them therefore observe how this happiness is mocked in ungodly men, and that all happiness is fixed unshakably in God alone. For they say blessed are the people to whom these things are; but blessed is the people whose Lord is their God. But they also thought that this was contrary to this passage of the Old Testament, in which the Lord says: Everyone who has confused me or my words in that adulterous and sinful nation, the Son of Man will also confuse him when he comes in the glory of his Father and the praise of his holy angels. I do not see that it belongs to the contempt of temporal things. But if it is for this reason, lest any, being afraid of the harms of such things, should be ashamed or afraid to confess Christ, what have they to say? Since we also say that these gifts of God are so, that they are still the lowest, and in comparison with the salutary

confession, not only to be lost, but also to be thrown away. it was promised by the Lord God.

Everything in the writings of both Testaments, both for seeking and for fleeing, and for taking and rejecting, are concordant and ordered according to their steps.

19. 1. Regarding what is written in the Law: I am the one who gives wealth to my friends and poverty to my enemies. To this sentence oppose that which the Lord says: Blessed are the poor in spirit, for theirs is the kingdom of heaven; and: Woe unto you that are rich, because you have received your comfort. But why do they not want to include other things in the Gospel? For where it is written: Blessed are the poor in spirit, for theirs is the kingdom of heaven; there he continues: Blessed are the meek, for they themselves shall inherit the earth. Behold, the friends of God have become rich by the inheritance of the earth. But when that rich man is reduced to such want, that he begs the poor man whom he had neglected to drop the moisture of his dry tongue with a finger dipped in water, let them understand how the poor become enemies of God, and know that this is what is written in the Law: I am the one who gives riches to my friends, and poverty to my enemies.

19. 2. For I have taught above that these temporal riches are despised in the old Scriptures, and he who chooses to read them will find them in innumerable places. Hence also the saying: A little is better for the just, than the riches of sinners are many. And that: The law of thy mouth is good to me, above thousands of gold and silver. And that: The true judgments of God, justified in the same, are much more desirable than gold and precious stones. And that: Blessed is the man who finds wisdom, and immortal who sees prudence. For it is better to buy it, than to buy treasures of gold and silver. But it is more precious than the best stones, no evil resists it; she is well known to all who approach her, and to those who consider her carefully. But everything that is precious is not worthy of him. And that: Because of this I wished, and understanding was given to me, and I called, and the spirit of wisdom came into me. And I put her before kingdoms and seats, and I took honesty to be nothing in comparison with her. Nor did I procure for him a precious stone: for all gold

is little sand in comparison with it, and silver will be esteemed as clay compared to it. If they had read these things, or had not read them impiously, they would have seen everything in the writings of both Testaments, both to seek and to flee, and to take and to reject, concordant with themselves and arranged according to their steps.

In the human nature, which by sin has flowed down into the lower parts, what God promises in figures to the carnal, he shows open to the spiritual.

20. 1. Regarding what is written in the Law: If you walk in the Law and keep my commandments; I will give the rains in their season, and the earth will bring forth its fruits, and the trees will bear fruit, and your vintages will succeed the harvests, and the harvest will be full of vintages. from your country; and pursue your enemies, and they shall fall before you by the sword. . You will eat the old that has grown old, and you will throw away the old before the new. Now no one must demand from us that we show these things in accordance with what God has promised to that people. For we have said many things about this matter, and to whom they are little, it is too late. However, what they say about the New Testament is contrary to this passage as well; namely, that which the Lord says: Do not carry gold, nor silver, nor coins in your belts; not a purse for the road, nor two coats, nor shoes, nor staff; for the laborer is worthy of his wages: what wonder if he gave these things to the Evangelist? Were the Jewish people called to this ministry? All this, however, must be examined spiritually, lest the Lord himself should appear to have done to ungodly men contrary to his commandments, who also had pockets in which he carried money for the necessary subsistence. Unless perhaps they are going to say that having money in the zones is a sin; but in the pockets, there should be no sin. Now that these were not commands, but permitted to the Apostles, is understood from this, that the Apostle Paul sought his livelihood by working with his own hands, and not by abusing that power, as he himself says, which the Lord gave to the Evangelists. For what is permitted by the Lord, it is also not permissible to do: but what is commanded, unless it is done, is a sin.

20. 2. They also add about that rich man, to whom God had said: Fool, I will demand your life from you this night; But what you have prepared, whose will

they be? and they say that it is no less contrary to this chapter of the Law: since in this the emptiness of vain joy is laughed at, because it regarded the uncertain as certain; and the omnipotence of the promiser made that promise certain to the people of Israel. Wherefore the Apostle Paul, writing to Timothy, speaks thus of the rich of this world, whom he knew to have their place among the members of the Church: Command the rich of this world, not to be wise in pride, nor to hope in the uncertainty of riches, but in the living God, who provides us with all things abundantly to to enjoy: let them do good, be rich in good works, give easily, share, lay up for themselves a good foundation for the future, so that they may grasp the true life. Who here does not understand that it is not guilty to have these things, but to love and hope in them, and to prefer or even contribute them to truth, justice, wisdom, faith, a good conscience, charity to God and neighbor, before all of whom the pious soul is rich in its secrets God's eyes? But that God may be loved, who bestows on those who love him all these things, both invisible and eternal, that is, he gives himself fully to all these things to his lovers: so that he himself may be loved, even at that time when the carnal soul, that is to say, entangled with the affections of the flesh, does not know how to long for anything but temporal things , he must be persuaded that God also gives these things to man; because it is both true and believed to be very useful. This was done to the people of Israel through those promises, which they sneer at the most ignorant wretched people, so that even in the lowest things, how could they learn to love God, although fear is more at work there. However, all these temporal gifts are figures of eternal gifts, and that victory over enemies foreshadows victory over the devil and his angels.

20. 3. And what these added, as if contrary to the Old Testament, which the Apostle speaks, that God is not pleased with strife and dissension, but with peace: let them know that such a God is preached in those Scriptures, from whom no one can take away his peace; not such as they themselves preach, who, fearing lest war should break into their regions, sent their members far away to endure foreign wars, and afterwards could not be freed and cleansed, defeated and defiled. But in human nature, which by sin has flowed down into lower things, God is so pleased with peace, that he does not leave the scales of justice, nor does he want the peace he loves to be trampled upon by sinners, but to be loved by those who contend, to be seized by conquerors, and to promise it in figurative form to the carnal, and to show it open to the spiritual.

It is not absurd that the curse was brought upon the old man, whom the Lord hangs on the tree.

21. Regarding what is written in Deuteronomy: Cursed is everyone who hangs on a tree. Although this question has often been aired by the Manichaeans, I do not see what is contrary to this opinion, which Adamantus thought to be opposed from the Gospel, where the Lord says: If you want to be perfect, sell all that you possess, and distribute to the poor, and take up your cross and follow me. . Apart from the fact that he mentions the cross, he does not pay attention to the fact that it is contrary to what was said: Cursed is everyone who hangs himself on a tree: as if anyone could take up such a cross and follow the Lord. But that is removed when we follow the Lord, of which the Apostle says: But those who are of Jesus Christ have crucified their flesh with passions and lusts. For by such a cross the old man, that is, the old life, which we drew from Adam, is destroyed, so that what was voluntary in him might become natural in us. This the apostle shows when he says: We were once by nature the children of wrath, just as the rest. If, then, the old life is from Adam, whence the old life is signified by the name of the old man; What is the absurdity of the fact that the curse was brought forward on the old man, whom the Lord hangs on the tree? Because from the very succession he bore mortality, being mortally born of the virgin Mary, having flesh that was not sinful, but still bearing the likeness of sinful flesh; because he could die, and death is from sin. Whence also it is said: Knowing that our old man was nailed to the cross together with him, that the body of sin might be emptied. It was not the Lord, therefore, through the tongue of Moses, the servant of God, but death itself deserved the curse, which our Lord, by receiving it, emptied. That death therefore hangs on the tree, which through the woman reached the man by the serpent's persuasion. Whence also the serpent, to signify death itself, was lifted up by Moses in the wilderness on a tree. And since we are healed from deadly lusts by faith in the cross of the Lord, by which cross death was hung on a tree; therefore those who were poisoned by the bites of snakes, on looking at the snake that was fixed and exalted in the tree, were immediately healed. The Lord Himself attested to this sacrament, saying: For as Moses lifted up the serpent in the wilderness, so must the Son of man be lifted up. But by accepting the most ignominious kind of death among men, our Lord Jesus Christ, that is, the death of the cross, commended his love to us, so that the apostle rightly said, igniting us in his

love: Christ redeemed us from the curse of the Law, becoming cursed for us. For it is written: Cursed is everyone who hangs on a tree. So that not only no death, but also no kind of death, Christian liberty should fear, like Jewish slavery.

As in the season of charity, so is the severity of God in the season of fear.

22. Of the man whom God commanded to be stoned, who was found gathering wood on the Sabbath. In the Gospel, when the Lord healed a man's dry hand on the Sabbath, he did a divine work, not a human one; He did not depart from his leisure who commanded and it was done. And therefore, it is not like this act of gathering wood, which when a man was found to do on the Sabbath, he was stoned to death by God's command. Much has already been said about the slavish observance of the Sabbath, and about the temporal revenge of death. For as in the time of charity goodness is most commended in the time of fear of God. And since it was not yet necessary before the coming of the Lord to expose to the people the legitimate sacraments of the figures, those men were not invited to understand the meaning, but were forced to fulfill the commandments: for they did not yet adhere to God through the spirit, but through the flesh they served the law. But I am surprised that these mourn the man who was stoned by the commandment of God, because he gathered wood contrary to the commandment of the Law, and they do not mourn the withered tree by the word of Christ, which had done no commandment; when they believe that the soul of a tree is like that of a man.

Fertility and continence.

23. Regarding what is written: Your wife is like a leafy vine, and your children like young olive trees around your table, and you will see your children's

children; and you will know that in this way the man who fears the Lord is blessed. This was said figuratively by the prophet, and the Manichaeans do not understand that it pertains to the meaning of the Church, and they think that it is the opposite of what the Lord says in the Gospel about swordsmen, who castrate themselves for the sake of the kingdom of heaven. But we have already discussed both the husband and the wife, and the swordsmen, as far as was sufficient, in the third chapter.

Man does not live by bread alone, but by every word of God.

24. Concerning what is written in Solomon: To imitate the ant, and to look at its care, because it gathers food for itself from the time of summer until the winter. Nor do the Manichaeans understand that this is to be taken spiritually, and they think that it is a commandment to lay up treasures on earth, or even to take care of these storehouses, which without any commandment many men hasten to fill. And therefore, Adimantus says from the Gospel that it is contrary to this sentence, where the Lord says: Do not think about tomorrow. But they do not understand that this pertains to that, so that we do not love temporal things, nor fear lest we lack what is necessary, and for the sake of obtaining them serve either God or men. For if this was said for the reason that bread should not be kept for the morrow, this is more fulfilled by the Roman wanderers, whom they call Passives, who give the daily provisions when their bellies are satisfied, or immediately give what remains, or throw them away, than even the disciples of the Lord, who are even with the Lord of heaven himself. and they had sacks when they walked on the ground; or Paul the Apostle, who despised all earthly things, yet so governed the things which were necessary for the present life, that he even commanded concerning widows, saying: If a faithful man has widows, he must give them enough, so that the Church may not be burdened, so that it may be sufficient for true widows. However, the word about the ant is so placed, that just as it gathers in the summer where it feeds in the winter, so every Christian in the tranquility of things, which is signified by summer, gathers the word of God, so that in adversity and tribulations, which are signified by the name of winter, he may have where he lives spiritually. For man does not live by bread alone, but by every word of God. But if this moves them, what the ant stores in the earth

what it gathers; let them also be angry with the treasure which the Lord says was found in the field.

What Adimantus put down from the Gospel is not inconsistent with the prophetic opinion.

25. Concerning what is written in Hosea: Give them an empty belly and dry breasts: kill the seed of their wombs, that they may not give birth. And this prophetic expression is of course figurative. For they also understand the belly not of the flesh in the Gospel, when they read: Rivers of living water flowed from his belly. And the apostle had certain breasts when he said: I gave you milk to drink, not meat; and again: I became a little one in your midst, as if a nurse were nursing her children. And the Galatians, declining to the carnal, give birth again, until Christ is formed in them. And therefore it is not inconsistent with this prophetic sentence that Adamantus laid down from the Gospel, that in the resurrection from the dead, they neither marry, nor take wives, nor die, but are like the angels of God. For this is certainly what the swordsmen receive, of whom Isaiah speaks: "A place named much better for sons and daughters, I will give them an eternal name," he says. Let them not think, therefore, that in the Gospel alone such a reward is promised to the saints: and an empty belly, and dry breasts, and a mortified seed, lest they should bring forth, let them understand that it was said of them of whom the apostle says: corrupted, reprobate concerning the faith: but they will no longer prosper; for their madness will be evident to all, just as it was theirs. When, therefore, they no longer prosper, then they will have an empty stomach, and dry breasts, and a mortified seed. In which opinion they are worthy to look at themselves as if in a mirror.

Evil is called twofold: one is what a man does, and the other is what he suffers.

26. Regarding what is written in the prophet Amos: If it is possible for two people walking on the road not to recognize each other at all, and for a lion to return to its cub without prey; if a bird falls to the ground without a bird, if they aim at a fly without reason, so that they catch nothing; if the trumpet shall

sound in the city, that the people may not be afraid: so also no evil shall be perpetrated in the city, which the Lord will not do. Evil in this context is not to be understood as sin, but as punishment. For evil is called doubly; One thing is what a man does, another is what he suffers: what he does is sin. what is suffered is punishment. Therefore the Prophet was talking about punishments when he said this. For divine providence controlling and governing all things, so that man does evil what he wills, so that he suffers evil what he does not want. And so they accuse the Prophet of saying these things, as if they had not read in the Gospel: Do not two sparrows come together, and one of them does not fall to the ground without the will of your Father? Thus, then, God does evil, which is not evil to God himself, but to those on whom he takes revenge. And so he himself, as far as it pertains to himself, does good; because all that is just is good, and that revenge is just. And therefore it is not contrary to what Adimantus objects that the Lord said: A good tree produces good fruits; but a bad tree produces bad fruit. For though hell be evil to the damned; yet God's justice is good, and the fruit itself is good from the tree. But because of the evils of his sins, he stores up for himself the wrath of God in the day of wrath and revelation of the just judgment of God, who will render to each one according to his works. Although these two trees are most obviously placed in the similitude of two men, that is, the just and the unjust: because unless each one changes his will, good cannot work. That it is placed in our power, he teaches in another place, where he says: Either make a good tree, and its fruit good; or make the tree evil, and its fruit evil. For he says this to those who thought they could speak good things when they were bad, that is, to make good fruit when the trees were bad. For thus he adds: Hypocrites, how can you speak good things when you are evil? An evil tree therefore cannot produce good fruit: but good can be made from evil, so that it may bring forth good fruit. For you were once darkness, says the Apostle; but now the light is in the Lord. It is as if he had said: You were once bad trees, and therefore you could not then produce anything but bad fruit; which follows by saying: Walk as children of light: for the fruit of light is in all righteousness and truth; proving what is acceptable to the Lord. For even in the very chapter of the Gospel, if Adamantus had not fled from the desire of malice, he might have observed how God is said to do evil. For the Lord said there, which he also mentioned: Every tree that does not bear good fruit will be cut down and thrown into the fire. These are the evils which God does, that is, punishments to sinners, that he will cast into the fire the trees which, persisting in wickedness, will not become good, since this is evil to the trees themselves. But God, as I have often said, does not give bad fruit, because the fruit of justice is the revenge of sin.

It is in our power to deserve either to be grafted in by God's goodness, or to be cut off by severity.

27. Concerning what is written in the prophet Isaiah: I am God who makes peace and decrees evil. This is also paid by the same rule. For Adamantus did not criticize that God said, I make peace; but what he said, I consider evil. When the Apostle Paul treated these two things in one place even more broadly, saying: You see then the goodness and severity of God: indeed, severity towards those who have fallen; but goodness is in you, if you continue in goodness: otherwise you too will be cut off, and if they do not continue in unbelief, they will be grafted in. For God is able to insert them again. In this apostolic discourse the goodness of God is sufficiently apparent, according to which Isaiah said: I am God who makes peace; and severity, according to what he said, I consider evil. At the same time, he also shows that it is in our power, that we deserve either to be grafted in by his goodness, or to be cut off by severity. It is not, therefore, a contrary Gospel to Isaiah, as Adamantus thinks, or rather wants it to be thought, where the Lord says: Blessed are the peacemakers, for they shall be called the children of God. Or, on the other hand, he had to recognize that even Isaiah knew that the children of God were peacemakers, because through him God said: I am the one who makes peace. But when he fixed his eye to misunderstand in one part, he blinded himself in the other. But if another blind man would like to say that the Old Testament is good, where God says: I do not want the death of a sinner, so much as that he return and live; and that the New Testament is bad, where Christ says: Go into the eternal fire, which has been prepared for the devil and his angels: would not, falling into the pit, all those who followed him, the uneducated and ignorant of the Scriptures, be plunged together with him into the blindness of ignorance, sprouting malice? But he who reads with a pious eye, and finds in the New Testament what they accuse in the Old, and in the Old what they praise in the New.

We admit that those things which are invisible to the eyes of the body are visible to the mind.

28. 1. Concerning what is written in Isaiah: And it came to pass in the year that King Uzziah died, I saw the Lord sitting on a very high seat; and the house of his glory was full, and around him stood the Seraphim, having old wings, and indeed they covered his face with two, and his feet with two. In this place, Adamantus opposes what the Apostle says: "But to the invisible King of the ages, honor and praise be for ever." In which question we must ask what he thought; or in that vision of Isaiah to pass over the two wings with which the Seraphim were flying, saying: Holy, holy, holy, Lord God of hosts: or not to say the whole in the words of the Apostle. For thus says the Apostle: But to the King of the ages, invisible, incorruptible, to God alone be honor and glory for ever and ever. Or perhaps he was afraid that the mention of the Trinity would commend the Prophet to the reader, and he might suspect that something great was lurking there? For it is said three times: Holy, holy, holy is the Lord God of hosts. But in the Apostle he perhaps saw that, if he had said, to the incorruptible God; he would be answered by what we now say to you: What, then, was the nation of darkness to do with the incorruptible God, if he did not want to fight with them? Either perhaps he read false manuscripts, or he is false where we read Diamondus himself, there is no need to discuss the doubtful matter any longer: but we must now ask how the Prophet said that he saw God in the highest seat, and the Apostle Paul said the truth, an invisible God. I therefore ask them whether the invisible can be seen. If they say they can; Why then are they slandered, if the Prophet saw the invisible God? But if they say that it is not possible, they will rather slander the Apostle himself, if they dare, who says: For the invisible things of God, from the constitution of the world, are seen understood by the things that have been made. For he himself said that they are invisible; and he again says, they are seen. Are they not forced here to admit that they are invisible to the bodily eyes, but visible to the mind? So therefore also the Prophet

He saw God, who is physically invisible, not physically, but spiritually.

28. 2. For many kinds of vision are found in the Holy Scriptures. One, according to the eyes of the body; as Abraham saw three men under the heather of Mambre, and Moses saw the fire in the bush, and the disciples transfigured the Lord on the mountain between Moses and Elias: and so on. Another, according to the spirit, by which we imagine those things which we feel through the body: for even when our own part is divinely assumed, many things are revealed, not through the eyes of the body, or the ears, or any other carnal sense; but still similar to these, as Peter saw that disc sent down from heaven with various animals. Of this kind also is that of Isaiah, which the ungodly criticize most impertinently. For God is not circumscribed by a corporeal form: but as many things are said figuratively, not literally; so also many things are shown figuratively. Now the third kind of vision is according to the intuition of the mind, by which, understood, truth and wisdom are seen: without which kind the two things which I have set forth before are either unfruitful, or even lead into error. For when those things which are divinely shown either to the bodily senses, or to that part of the soul which perceives the images of corporeal things, are not only felt in these ways, but are also understood by the mind, then the revelation is complete. Of this third kind is that vision which I mentioned, when the Apostle said: For the invisible things of God, from the constitution of the world, are seen understood by the things that have been made. In this vision God is seen, when hearts are purified by the piety of faith and by the recognition of God's best manners. For what benefited King Balthasar when he saw the hand writing before his eyes on the wall? Since he could not attach the mental aspect to that vision, he still sought to see what he had seen. Daniel, endowed with such a line of light by which these things are understood, saw with his mind what he had seen with his body. Again, with that part of the mind which receives the images of bodies, King Nebuchadnezzar saw a dream: and since he did not have the mind's eye suitable to see better what he had seen, that is, to understand what he had seen, therefore to interpret his vision, he sought an alien vision, namely that of Daniel: but to whom the opener, in order to accommodate a certain faith, even required the dream itself to be told to him. But Daniel, being revealed by the Holy Spirit of God, and what he had seen in dreams, he saw in that part where the images of bodies are taken, and he saw what it signified in his mind. Now he is not a prophet of the truth of God and of the Most High, who sees the divine offerings, either with the body alone, or even with that part of the spirit in which the images of bodies are taken, and does not see with the mind. But

generally in the Scriptures they are found thus placed, as they were seen, not even as they were understood; so that the vision of the mind, in which the whole fruit is, may be preserved by exercising the readers. But from many things which are plainly written, it is made manifest to us how they understood those things, which they thus set down in books, how they were shown to them figuratively. For to these two kinds of vision belong figurative demonstrations: but to the vision of the mind, that is, to the vision of the understanding, belongs the simple and proper revelation of things understood and certain. All these kinds, however, are presented and controlled by the Holy Spirit of supreme and unchangeable wisdom in wonderful and ineffable distributions. But wretched are those who slander the Prophet by saying that he sees God, objecting to the apostolic opinion, where he said invisible. For if another object to this apostolic word is the evangelical word, in which the Lord says: Blessed are the hearts of the world, for they shall see God; How will they answer that the invisible can be seen? For with the word, they oppress the ignorant, and inasmuch as God is said to be invisible, though they know, they fear to be known. Such is the perdition of minds which, when they want to conquer a man, are conquered by error.

LATIN TEXT

CONTRA ADIMANTUM MANICHAEI DISCIPULUM

1. 1. De eo quod scriptum est: In principio fecit Deus coelum et terram; usque ad id quod scriptum est: Et factum est vespere, et factum est mane dies unus. Hoc capitulum Legis adversum esse Evangelio stultissimi Manichaei arbitrantur, dicentes in Genesi scriptum esse quod Deus per se ipsum fecerit coelum et terram et lucem; in Evangelio autem scriptum esse per Dominum nostrum Iesum Christum fabricatum esse mundum, ubi dictum est: Et mundus per ipsum factus est, et mundus illum non cognovit. Tribus enim modis refelluntur. Primo, quia cum dicitur: In principio fecit Deus coelum et terram; Trinitatem ipsam christianus accipit, ubi non solum Pater, sed et Filius et Spiritus sanctus intellegitur. Non enim tres deos, sed unum Deum credimus, Patrem et Filium et Spiritum sanctum: quamvis Pater Pater, et Filius Filius sit, et Spiritus sanctus Spiritus sanctus. De qua unitate Trinitatis hoc loco longum est disputare. Deinde, quia ubi dicitur: Dixit Deus: Fiat, et factum est; ibi necesse est intellegatur per Verbum eum fecisse quod fecit. Verbum autem Patris est Filius. Non ergo repugnat hoc capitulum Geneseos, ubi scriptum est: Et Dixit Deus: Fiat, et factum est; illi loco Evangelii ubi dicitur: Et mundus per eum factus est, id est, per Dominum nostrum; quia ipse est Verbum Patris per quod facta sunt omnia. Postremo, si propterea in Genesi non intellegitur Filius, quia non est dictum quod per Filium Deus fecerit; nec in Evangelio per Filium Deus et aves pascit, et lilia vestit, et cetera innumerabilia quae ipse Dominus dicit Deum facere Patrem: quamvis non dicat quod ea per Filium faciat. Quod autem etiam testimonium Apostoli adiungunt, quod ait de Domino nostro Iesu Christo: Ipse est primogenitus totius creaturae; et omnia per ipsum facta sunt in coelo et in terra, visibilia et invisibilia; et hoc capitulum adversum esse dicunt Genesi, ubi Deus ita dicitur fecisse mundum, ut specialiter Filius ibi non sit nominatus: vehementer errant; et non vident, si ita est, ipsum Apostolum sibi esse contrarium, cum alio loco unum dicit, ex quo omnia, per quem omnia, in quo omnia; et Filium non nominat. Quomodo autem hic Filius nominatus non est, intellegitur tamen; ita et in Genesi: et quomodo sibi haec duo capitula Pauli non adversantur; ita nec Genesis Evangelio.

AGAINST ADIMANTUS, DISCIPLE OF MANICHAEUS

Manichaei dicunt Novo Testamento adversari quod in Genesi scriptum est, Deum septimo die requievisse.

2. 1. De eo quod scriptum est: Et consummavit Deus die sexto omnia opera sua quae fecit, et in septimo requievit ab eisdem omnibus operibus quae fecerat. Huic etiam loco Manichaei calumniam movent, et dicunt Novo Testamento adversari quod in Genesi scriptum est, Deum septimo die requievisse ab omnibus operibus suis quae fecit: quoniam Dominus in Evangelio dicit: Pater meus usque nunc operatur. Quod nullo modo contrarium est. Dominus enim Iudaeorum refellit errorem, qui putabant Deum sic requievisse die septimo, ut ex illo prorsus nihil operaretur. Requievit autem ab omnibus operibus suis quae fecit, ut iam ultra non faceret mundum cum omnibus quae in eo sunt: non tamen ut etiam a mundi administratione requiesceret. Non enim scriptum est: Requievit Deus ab omnibus operibus suis, ut deinceps non operaretur. Sed scriptum est: Requievit Deus ab omnibus operibus suis quae fecit: ut deinde non in faciendo mundo, a quo opere post perfectionem cessaverat; sed in administrando operaretur, in quo opere eum esse Dominus intimavit. Nec illa requies, quasi post laborem Deum pausam quaesisse, sed ab instituendis rerum naturis post earum rerum perfectionem cessasse significat, quamvis usque adhuc in administrandis operetur.

Sabbatum non repudiatum, sed intellectum a Christianis.

2. 2. Sabbati autem observationem non intellegebant Iudaei, qui putabant ab iis etiam operibus quae ad salutem hominum valent, oportere cessari. Unde illos Dominus etiam aliis locis, de bove qui in puteum cecidit, et iumento quod solvendum est ut ad aquam ducatur, mirifica comparatione redarguit. Sabbatum autem, non repudiatum, sed intellectum a Christianis destitit quidem carnaliter observari, sed spiritaliter retinetur a sanctis, qui intellegunt vocem Domini vocantis ad requiem, et dicentis: Venite ad me, qui laboratis, et ego vos reficiam. Tollite iugum meum super vos, et discite a me quia mitis sum et humilis corde, et invenietis requiem animabus vestris. Iugum enim meum lene est, et sarcina mea levis est. Hoc sabbatum, id est, hanc requiem Scriptura illa significat, quam Iudaei non intellegebant, et pro temporum dispensatione carnaliter sequebantur umbram, cuius umbrae quasi corpus, id est, veritas

nobis danda erat. Sed quemadmodum illa requies Dei post fabricatum mundum insinuatur; sic requiem, quae nobis promittitur, post opera quae in hoc mundo habemus, si iusta fuerint, consequemur, septima scilicet eademque ultima parte saeculi, de qua longum est disputare. Non ergo Dominus rescindit scripturam Veteris Testamenti, sed cogit intellegi: nec sabbatum solvit ut pereat quod figurabatur, sed aperit potius ut appareat quod tegebatur.

Manichaei dicunt contra Novum Testamentum esse istam sententiam, qua Deus scribitur et formasse mulierem, et viro coniunxisse.

3. 1. De eo quod scriptum est in Genesi: Et dixit Deus: Non est bonum solum hominem esse; faciamus ei adiutorium. Et immisit Deus Adae somnum, et obdormivit; et sumpsit unam de costis eius, ex qua formavit Evam, quam adduxit ad Adam; et ait: Ideo relinquet homo patrem et matrem, et adhaerebit uxori suae. Huic rursus loco Manichaei calumniantur, dicentes contra Novum Testamentum esse istam sententiam, qua Deus scribitur et formasse mulierem, et viro coniunxisse: propterea, quia in Evangelio dicit Dominus: Omnis qui reliquerit domum, aut uxorem, aut parentes, aut fratres, aut filios propter regnum coelorum, centies tantum accipiet in hoc tempore, et in futuro saeculo possidebit vitam aeternam. In qua calumnia miror eos sic esse caecatos, vel potius non miror: Excaecavit enim illos, sicut scriptum est, malitia eorum. Sed tamen quis non videt tanta in Novo Testamento praecepta de uxore diligenda? Cur enim potius Vetus Testamentum dicunt adversari huic sententiae Domini, qua dicit relinquendam esse uxorem propter regnum coelorum, et non ipsum Novum sibi adversari? Quod nefas est dicere. Intellegenda enim sunt, non temere accusanda, quae imperitis videntur esse contraria.

3. 2. Nam et Dominus interrogatus a Iudaeis, utrum ei placeret dato libello repudii dimittere uxorem, respondit eis dicens: Non legistis quoniam qui fecit ab initio, masculum et feminam fecit eos; et dixit: Propter hoc relinquet homo patrem et matrem, et adhaerebit uxori suae, et erunt duo in carne una? Itaque iam non sunt duo, sed una caro. Quod ergo Deus coniunxit in unum, homo non separet. Dicunt illi: Quid ergo Moyses mandavit dari libellum repudii, et dimittere? Dicit illis Iesus: Quia ad duritiam cordis vestri permisit vobis Moyses dimittere uxores vestras; ab initio autem non fuit sic. Dico autem vobis,

quicumque dimiserit uxorem suam, nisi ob causam fornicationis, facit eam moechari: et ipse si alteram duxerit, adulterium committit. Ecce habent confirmatam sententiam Veteris Testamenti ab ipso Domino adversus imperitiam Iudaeorum. Simul etiam Moysi perhibuit testimonium, quod propter duritiam cordis eorum repudium dari permisit. Numquid etiam Evangelium Evangelio dicunt esse contrarium? Quod si dicunt hoc capitulum falsum esse, et a corruptoribus Scripturarum esse additum (nam hoc solent, quando non inveniunt quid respondeant, dicere); quid, si alius dicat illud esse immissum et falsum, quod ipsi proferunt dicente Domino: Omnis qui reliquerit domum aut uxorem aut parentes aut filios propter regnum coelorum, et cetera? Non intellegunt miseri quemadmodum omnem fidem christianam, cum ista dicunt, conentur evertere. Fides autem vera et Ecclesiae catholicae disciplina utrumque verum et a Domino dictum esse confirmat, et nullo modo esse contrarium: quia et coniunctio mariti et uxoris a Domino est, et relictio uxoris propter regnum coelorum a Domino est. Non enim quia suscitavit Iesus Christus mortuos, et dedit eis vitam, propterea ipsa vita non est relinquenda propter regnum coelorum. Sic ergo quamvis Dominus dederit uxorem viro, relinquenda est tamen, si opus est, propter regnum coelorum. Non enim hoc semper necesse est, sicut Apostolus dicit: Si quis fidelis habet uxorem infidelem, et haec consentit habitare cum illo, non dimittat eam. Significat utique quod si non consentit habitare cum illo, id est, si exsecratur in illo fidem Christi, et non eum patitur, quod christianus est, relinquenda est propter regnum coelorum, sicut idem apostolus in sequentibus dicit: Quod si infidelis discedit, discedat; non est enim subiectus servituti frater aut soror in huiusmodi. Si quis ergo relinquit regnum coelorum, dum non vult relinquere uxorem non ferentem christianum virum, improbatur a Domino: et item si quis vir relinquit uxorem dato libello repudii, cum causa non existit aut fornicationis, aut obtinendi regni coelorum, similiter improbatur a Domino. Ita nec ista duo capitula evangelica inveniuntur sibi esse contraria, nec Evangelium Veteri Testamento: quia ibi uxor coniungitur viro, ut simul mereantur possidere regnum coelorum; et ita uxor relinquenda esse praecipitur, si virum impediat ad possidendum regnum coelorum.

3. 3. Et ideo quando Christianos utrosque Apostolus monet, id est, maritos et uxores; nonne ita dicitur: Diligite uxores vestras, sicut et Christus dilexit Ecclesiam, et tradidit se ipsum pro ea? et: Mulieres viris suis subditae sint quasi

Domino; quia et Ecclesia subdita est Christo? Nonne illud quod isti miseri irrident in Veteri Testamento, quod scriptum est: Propterea relinquet homo patrem et matrem, et adhaerebit uxori suae, et erunt duo in carne una, in magno sacramento idem apostolus accipit, cum dicit: Sacramentum hoc magnum est, ego autem dico in Christo et in Ecclesia? Deinde subiungit: Verumtamen unusquisque uxorem suam sicut se ipsum diligat; mulier autem ut timeat virum. Nonne alio loco evidentissime ostendit utriusque sexus et naturam et coniunctionem a Domino Deo conditore atque ordinatore consistere, cum dicit: Verumtamen neque mulier sine viro, neque vir sine muliere, in Domino. Sicut enim mulier ex viro, ita et vir per mulierem: omnia autem ex Deo? Quod isti si considerare vellent, non quibusdam capitulis separatis et adversus se invicem magna fraude collatis caliginem facerent imperitis; sed omnia tam in Veteri quam in Novo Testamento uno sancto Spiritu conscripta et commendata esse sentirent.

3. 4. Nam et in Veteri Testamento habent apud Isaiam prophetam quanta promittantur spadonibus: ne in Novo solo arbitrentur esse laudatos a Domino, ubi dicit esse quosdam qui se ipsos castraverunt propter regnum coelorum, et addidit: Qui potest capere, capiat. Nam et Isaias ita dicit: Haec dicit Dominus spadonibus eis qui custodierint praecepta mea, et elegerint sibi quae ego volo, et capaces fuerint testamenti mei; dabo illis in domo mea et in muro meo locum nominatissimum, meliorem multo filiorum atque filiarum: nomen aeternum dabo illis, nec umquam deerit. Certis enim quibusdam umbris et figuris rerum ante Domini adventum, secundum mirabilem atque ordinatissimam distributionem temporum, populus ille tenebatur, qui Testamentum Vetus accepit: tamen in eo tanta praedicatio et praenuntiatio Novi Testamenti est, ut nulla in evangelica atque apostolica disciplina reperiantur, quamvis ardua et divina praecepta et promissa, quae illis etiam Libris veteribus desint. Sed sanctae Scripturae non temerarios et superbos accusatores, sed diligentes et pios lectores desiderant.

Capitulo Geneseos, quo maledictionem accepit Cain, ut terrae sterilitate puniretur, calumniantes Manichaei, et Evangelio contrarium demonstrare cupientes.

4. De eo quod scriptum est in Genesi: Et dixit Dominus ad Cain: Quid fecisti? Vox sanguinis fratris tui clamat ad me de terra. Nunc maledictus eris a facie terrae, quae absorbuit et recepit sanguinem fratris tui ex caede manus tuae: te enim operari necesse est terram, quae steriles tibi fructus dabit. Huic capitulo Geneseos, quo maledictionem accepit Cain, ut terrae sterilitate puniretur, calumniantes Manichaei, et Evangelio contrarium demonstrare cupientes, non sane, mihi videntur cogitare cum hominibus se agere, sed prorsus quasi pecora forent, qui eos audirent vel eorum scripta legerent; sic abusi sunt imperitia eorum et tarditate ingenii, vel potius animi caecitate. Quippe dixerunt huic capitulo illud in Evangelio esse contrarium, quod Dominus ait discipulis suis: Nolite cogitare de crastino; nam crastinus dies ipse cogitabit sibi. Respicite volatilia coeli, quia non seminant, neque metunt, neque colligunt in horrea. Quasi vero Cain parricida discipulis Christi comparandus sit, ut quoniam ille meruit poenam sterilitatis terrae, consequens esset ut eamdem sterilitatem isti etiam paterentur, qui Dominum Iesum Christum secuti, praedicando Evangelio parabantur. Imo etiam in istis duobus capitulis, quorum unum de Genesi, alterum de Evangelio tamquam sibi inimica posuerunt, tanta invenitur amicitia atque concordia, ut nulla maior desideranda sit. Quid enim congruentius, quid convenientius quam ut illum, cuius erat scelere frater occisus, etiam in terra laborantem sterilitas sequeretur: illis autem, per quorum ministerium in praedicando Dei verbo fratres liberabantur, etiam de crastino minime cogitantibus fructuosa terra serviret? Quod si in Veteri Testamento exhorrescunt maledicto Dei terram sterilem factam esse peccatori; cur non in Novo Testamento exhorrescunt maledicto Domini nostri Iesu Christi arborem fici aridam factam, nullo peccato domini sui? Item si Domini sententia delectantur, qua discipulis dicit ne de crastino cogitent, quod de victu eorum Deus curam gerat; cur non et prophetica sententia delectantur, qua cecinit dicens: Abice in Dominum sollicitudinem tuam, et ipse te pascet? Ut hoc modo, si possint, miseri intellegant, et illa quae detestantur in Veteri Testamento de Deo dicta, usque adeo recta esse, ut etiam in Novo inveniantur; et illa quae in Novo laudant et praedicant, etiam in Veteri reperiri: unde clarescat bene intellegentibus utriusque Testamenti manifesta concordia.

Ad imaginem Dei factum hominem, non tantum Genesis, sed etiam Apostolus clamat.

5. 1. De eo quod scriptum est in Genesi: Faciamus hominem ad imaginem et similitudinem nostram. Hunc locum Manichaei, quo scriptum est in Genesi, hominem factum esse ad imaginem et similitudinem Dei, propterea dicunt Novo Testamento esse contrarium, quia Dominus in Evangelio dicit Iudaeis: Vos ex patre diabolo estis, et desideria patris vestri facere vultis: ille homicida erat ab initio, et in veritate non stetit, quia veritas in eo non est, et quod alio loco Iudaei serpentum genimina et viperarum appellantur. Non intellegunt illud esse dictum de homine antequam peccaret, quod factus est ad imaginem et similitudinem Dei; hoc autem quod in Evangelio est: Vos ex patre diabolo estis, peccatoribus et infidelibus dici. Tribus enim modis in Scripturis sanctis filiorum nomen accipitur: uno, secundum naturam, quomodo Isaac filius Abrahae, vel etiam ceteri Iudaei qui ex eadem origine veniunt; alio, secundum doctrinam, ut filius eius in ea re quisque appelletur, a quo aliquid didicit; sicut filios suos Apostolus appellat, qui ab illo didicerunt Evangelium; tertio, secundum imitationem, sicut filios Abrahae nos vocat Apostolus, qui eius fidem imitamur. Duobus ergo modis peccatores infideles Iudaei, filii diaboli vocantur a Domino; vel quod ab ipso impietatem didicerunt, sicut de ipso diabolo Apostolus dicit: Qui nunc operatur in filiis diffidentiae; vel quod eum imitantur, quod magis pertinet ad id quod de illo dictum est: Et in veritate non stetit; quia et ipsi Iudaei in veritate legis quae sibi data est, non steterunt, Domino attestante et dicente: Si crederetis Moysi, crederetis et mihi: ille enim de me scripsit. Secundum eorumdem peccatorum venena etiam serpentum et viperarum genimina vocantur.

5. 2. Ad imaginem autem Dei factum hominem, non tantum Genesis, sed etiam Apostolus clamat, cum dicit: Vir quidem non debet velare caput, cum sit imago et gloria Dei, mulier autem gloria viri. Et ut manifeste intellegatur non secundum vetustatem peccati quae corrumpitur, sed secundum spiritalem conformationem factum esse hominem ad imaginem Dei, idem apostolus monet ut exuti consuetudine peccatorum, id est, vetere homine, induamur nova vita Christi, quem novum hominem appellat. Et ut doceat hoc nos aliquando amisisse, renovationem illam vocat. Nam ita loquitur: Exspoliantes vos veterem hominem cum actibus eius, induite novum, qui renovatur in agnitionem Dei, secundum imaginem eius qui creavit eum. Filii ergo Dei sunt homines renovati ad eius imaginem, et ei similes facti usque ad dilectionem inimici: sicut Dominus dicit, diligere nos debere inimicos nostros, ut similes

simus Patri nostro qui in coelis est. Quod in potestate nostra ab ipso Deo esse positum docet Scriptura, cum dicit: Dedit eis potestatem filios Dei fieri. Filii autem diaboli dicuntur homines, cum imitantur eius impiam superbiam, et a luce atque celsitudine sapientiae decidunt, et non credunt veritati; quales Dominus arguit, cum dicit: Vos ex patre diabolo estis, et cetera. Cui loco evangelico propheta consonat, dicens: Ego dixi: Dii estis, et filii Altissimi omnes; vos autem ut homines moriemini, et sicut unus ex principibus cadetis.

Et parentes honorare debemus, et eos tamen propter annuntiationem regni Dei nulla impietate contemnimus.

6. De eo quod scriptum est in Exodo: Honora patrem tuum, et matrem tuam. Huic etiam loco, ubi de honorandis parentibus Deus praecepit, illum Evangelii locum Manichaei dicunt esse contrarium, ubi Dominus cuidam dicenti: Ibo primum ut sepeliam patrem meum; respondit: Sine mortuos, mortuos suos sepeliant; tu autem veni, et annuntia regnum Dei. Quod eodem modo solvitur, quo illud superius, ubi de uxore relinquenda dictum est: Propter regnum coelorum; quia et parentes honorare debemus, et eos tamen propter annuntiationem regni Dei nulla impietate contemnimus. Nam si Veteri Testamento contrarium est Evangelium propter istam sententiam, incipit etiam Apostolo esse contrarium, qui et filios monet ut honorent parentes, et parentes ut diligant filios. Non solum autem, sed etiam Dominus videbitur sibi ipsi esse contrarius (quod credere nefas est), quia loco alio dicit homini quaerenti vitam aeternam: Si vis venire ad vitam, serva mandata, in quibus etiam illud commemorat: Honora patrem et matrem. Quibus mandatis perfectis etiam ad dilectionem Dei crescitur, in qua est tota perfectio. Nam dilectio proximi certus gradus est ad dilectionem Dei. Et ideo respondenti quod omnia mandata illa servavit, dicit unum ei deesse, si vult esse perfectus, ut vendat omnia quae habet, et det pauperibus, et sequatur eum. Ex quo manifestum est, et honorem parentum in gradu suo esse servandum, et eos tamen in divini amoris comparatione, praesertim si impedimento sunt, nulla dubitatione oportere contemni. Nam et in Scripturis veteribus habes positum: Qui dicit patri aut matri: Non novi vos, et qui filios suos non agnoscit, ipse autem cognovit testamentum tuum. Ergo si et in Novo Testamento commendatur parentum dilectio, et in Veteri commendatur parentum contemptus, ex utroque capite duo sibi Testamenta consentiunt.

Qua concordia utriusque Testamenti satis ostenditur non esse saevum Deum, sed unumquemque in se saevire peccando.

7. 1. De eo quod in Exodo scriptum est: Ego sum Deus zelans, tribuens filiis tertiae et quartae generationis parentum peccata qui me oderunt. Huic loco Manichaei illud de Evangelio dicunt esse contrarium, quod Dominus dicit: Estote benigni sicut Pater vester coelestis, qui solem suum oriri facit super bonos et malos, et illud aliud quod idem Dominus ait: Non solum septies peccanti fratri dimittendum, sed etiam septuagies septies. A quibus tamen si quaeram utrum Deus non puniat inimicos suos, sine dubio turbabuntur. Ipsi enim dicunt: Deum genti tenebrarum aeternum carcerem praeparare, quam dicunt esse inimicam Deo. Et parum est, sed eum etiam sua membra simul cum ipsa gente puniturum esse non dubitant dicere. Sed cum ad capitula Veteris et Novi Testamenti veniunt, ut imperitos decipiant, et ea sibi adversa esse criminentur, fingunt se nimis bonos. Sed dicant nobis, quibus dicturus est Dominus: Ite in ignem aeternum, qui praeparatus est diabolo et angelis eius; si omnibus parcit et neminem damnat? Quare intellegendum est et illud rectum esse, quod Deus retribuit parentum peccata filiis qui eum oderunt. Ex eo enim quod addidit, qui me oderunt, intellegitur eos puniri peccatis parentum, qui in eadem perversitate parentum perseverare voluerunt. Tales enim non saevitia, sed potius iustitia Dei, et sua iniquitate puniuntur, sicut Propheta ait: Sanctus enim Spiritus disciplinae effugiet fictum, et auferet se a cogitationibus quae sunt sine intellectu, et corripietur a superveniente iniquitate, id est, corripietur homo superveniente sibi iniquitate sua, cum ab eo recesserit Spiritus sanctus. Et alio loco: Haec cogitaverunt, et erraverunt; excaecavit enim illos malitia eorum. Et alio loco: Funiculis peccatorum suorum unusquisque constringitur. Quibus testimoniis veteris Testamenti de Novo consentit Apostolus dicens: Tradidit illos Deus in concupiscentias cordis eorum. Qua concordia utriusque Testamenti satis ostenditur non esse saevum Deum, sed unumquemque in se saevire peccando.

7. 2. Quod autem in tertiam et quartam scriptum est generationem vindictam procedere, non aliud significari arbitror, nisi quod ab ipso Abraham, qui pater esse incipit populi Iudaeorum, quatuor aetates sunt cum ista quae nunc agitur, quas Matthaeus evangelista distinguit. Una est ab Abraham usque ad David: alia, a David usque ad transmigrationem in Babyloniam: tertia, a

transmigratione in Babyloniam usque ad Domini adventum: inde usque ad finem quarta deputatur, tamquam senectus saeculi ceteris aetatibus longior. Quas aetates pro generationibus positas credimus, quamvis singulae pluribus generationibus constent. Et quoniam tertia incipit a transmigratione Babyloniae, quando Iudaeorum est facta captivitas; in quarta vero, id est, post adventum Domini nostri, gens Iudaeorum a solo proprio penitus eradicata est: hoc datur intellegi quod dictum est, tertiae et quartae generationis peccata parentum redditurum Deum, his utique legitime atque debite, qui parentum peccata perseverantes tenere, quam Dei iustitiam sequi maluerunt. Nam non pertinere patris peccata ad filium iuste viventem, propheta Ezechiel apertissime ostendit.

7. 3. Quod autem in Evangelio dicitur: Estote benigni quemadmodum Pater vester coelestis, qui solem suum oriri facit super bonos et malos; non est Veteri Testamento contrarium. Hoc enim facit Deus ut invitet ad poenitentiam, sicut dicit Apostolus: Ignoras quia patientia Dei ad poenitentiam te invitat? Nec tamen ideo credendum est non puniturum Deum eos, qui, ut dicit idem Apostolus, thesaurizant sibi iram in die irae, et revelationis iusti iudicii Dei, qui reddet unicuique secundum opera sua. Namque istam Dei patientiam et bonitatem etiam Propheta praedicat, dicens: Parcis autem omnibus, quoniam tua sunt omnia, qui animas amas, et cetera innumerabilia quibus intellegitur et in bonitate et in severitate misericordiam et iustitiam Dei Testamentum utrumque praedicare.

7. 4. Si autem moventur quod dictum est: Ego sum zelans; moveantur etiam illo quod dicit apostolus Paulus: Zelo Dei vos zelo; desponsavi enim vos uni viro virginem castam exhibere Christo. Sancta enim Scriptura verbis nostris loquens, etiam per haec verba demonstrat, nihil digne de Deo posse dici. Cur enim non etiam verba ista dicantur de illa maiestate, de qua quidquid dictum fuerit, indigne dicitur; quia omnes opes linguarum omnium ineffabili sublimitate praecedit? Nam quoniam zelando solent mariti uxorum pudicitiam custodire, potestatem et disciplinam Dei, qua fornicari animam impune non sinit, zelum Dei Scripturae vocaverunt. Est autem animae fornicatio, aversio a fecunditate sapientiae, et ad conceptum temporalium illecebrarum corruptionumque conversio.

7. 5. Illud vero quod dimittendum esse dicit fratri, non solum septies, sed et septuagies septies, poenitenti utique dicit. Deus autem illis se dicit retribuere peccata, qui eum oderunt, non qui ei per poenitentiam reconciliantur. Nam et apud prophetam Dominus dicit: Nolo mortem peccatoris quantum ut revertatur et vivat. Ex quo facile apparet, et in ea patientia quae invitat ad poenitentiam, et in ea indulgentia quae ignoscit poenitentibus, et in ea iustitia quae punit eos qui corrigi nolunt, utrumque Testamentum sibi convenire atque congruere, tamquam ab uno Deo utrumque conscriptum.

Mensura vindicandi recte carnalibus constituta; sed omnimoda iniuriae remissio, non tantum in Novo Testamento est praecepta, sed longe ante in Vetere praenuntiata.

8. De eo quod scriptum est in Exodo: Oculum pro oculo, dentem pro dente; et cetera talia. Huic loco Manichaei, quod in veteri Lege par vindicta permittitur, et dicitur oculum pro oculo, dentem pro dente esse perdendum, sic calumniantur, quasi et ipse Dominus haec duo sibi veluti adversantia atque contraria in Evangelio demonstraverit. Ipse enim ait: Audistis quia dictum est antiquis: Oculum pro oculo, et dentem pro dente; ego autem dico vobis, non resistere malo; sed si quis te percusserit in maxillam, praebe illi et alteram; et quicumque voluerit tecum iudicio contendere, et tunicam tuam auferre, dimitte illi et pallium. In quibus duabus sententiis revera duorum Testamentorum differentia demonstratur, sed amborum tamen ab uno Deo constitutorum. Nam quoniam primo carnales homines ardebant multo amplius se vindicare, quam erat illa iniuria, de qua querebantur, constitutus est eis primus lenitatis gradus, ut iniuriae acceptae mensuram nullo modo dolor vindicantis excederet. Sic enim et donare aliquando posset iniuriam, qui eam primo non superare didicisset. Unde Dominus iam per Evangelii gratiam ad summam pacem populum deducens, huic gradui superaedificavit alterum; ut qui iam audierat non ampliorem vindictam, quam quisque laesus esset, reddere, placata mente totum se donare gauderet. Quod etiam in illis veteribus Libris Propheta praedicat, dicens: Domine Deus meus, si feci istud, si est iniquitas in manibus meis, si reddidi retribuentibus mihi mala. Et alius propheta dicit de huiusmodi viro patiente iniurias, et lenissime tolerante: Dabit percutienti se maxillam, saturabitur opprobriis. Ex quo intelligitur et mensuram vindicandi recte carnalibus constitutam, et omnimodam iniuriae remissionem, non

tantum in Novo Testamento esse praeceptam, sed longe ante in Vetere praenuntiatam.

Ex utroque Testamento de Deo visibili et de Deo invisibili omnia testimonia consonant.

9. 1. De eo quod scriptum est, quod locutus est Deus cum Adam et Eva, et cum serpente, et cum Cain, et ceteris antiquis: inter quos etiam et nonnullis apparuisse scribitur, et ab eis visus esse, non uno, sed multis Scripturarum locis, in quibus et locutus esse Deus cum hominibus invenitur, et nonnullis apparuisse: insidiantur Manichaei, et dicunt omnia contraria esse Novo Testamento, quoniam Dominus dicit: Deum nemo vidit umquam, nisi unicus Filius, qui est in sinu Patris; ille annuntiavit nobis de eo; et iterum quod dicit Iudaeis: Nec vocem illius aliquando audistis, nec faciem eius vidistis, nec verbum eius habetis in vobis manens: quia ei quem ille misit, non credidistis. Quibus respondemus eo ipso, quod in Evangelio scriptum est: Deum nemo vidit unquam, nisi unicus Filius qui est in sinu Patris; ipse annuntiavit nobis de eo, totam ipsam solvi posse quaestionem: quia ipse Filius, quod est Verbum Dei, non solum novissimis temporibus, cum in carne apparere dignatus est, sed etiam prius a constitutione mundi, cui voluit de Patre annuntiavit, sive loquendo, sive apparendo, vel per angelicam aliquam potestatem, vel per quamlibet creaturam: quia ipse est in omnibus veritas, et omnia illi constant, et omnia illi ad nutum serviunt, atque subiecta sunt; ut etiam oculis per visibilem creaturam cui vult, quando dignatur, appareat: cum ipse tamen secundum divinitatem suam, et secundum id quod Verbum est Patris, coaeternum Patri, et incommutabile, per quod facta sunt omnia, non nisi purgatissimo et simplicissimo corde videatur. Et ideo quibusdam locis etiam Scriptura ipsa testatur angelum visum, ubi dicit Deum visum. Sicut in illa luctatione Iacob, et angelus dictus est ille qui apparuit. Et cum apparuit in rubo Moysi; et item in eremo, cum iam eduxisset populum de terra Aegypti, quando legem accepit, Deus ei locutus est. Sed sive in rubo, cum eum misit; sive postea, cum ei legem dedit, angelum dicit Stephanus in Actibus Apostolorum ei apparuisse. Quod ideo dicimus, ne quis arbitretur Verbum Dei, per quod facta sunt omnia, quasi per locos posse definiri, et alicui visibiliter apparere, nisi per aliquam visibilem creaturam. Sicut enim Verbum Dei est in propheta, et recte dicitur: Dixit Propheta, recte item dicitur: Dixit Dominus; quia Verbum Dei, quod est

Christus, in propheta loquitur veritatem: sic et in angelo ipse loquitur, quando veritatem angelus annuntiat; et recte dicitur: Deus dixit; et: Deus apparuit; et item dicitur recte: Angelus dixit, et: Angelus apparuit; cum illud dicatur ex persona inhabitantis Dei, illud ex persona servientis creaturae. Ex hac regula etiam

Apostolus ait: An vultis experimentum eius accipere, qui in me loquitur Christi?

9. 2. Si autem hoc movet, quod in Veteri Testamento etiam peccatoribus Deus loquitur, vel Adae vel Evae, vel serpenti; attendant etiam in Novo cuiusmodi exemplum Dominus posuit de homine stulto et cupido, quomodo ei locutus est Dominus, cum ait: Stulte, hac nocte auferetur a te anima tua; haec quae praeparasti cuius erunt? Cum enim veritas etiam peccatoribus dicitur, per quamlibet creaturam dicatur, non nisi ab illo dicitur, qui unus est verax. Quod autem Iudaeis dicit: Nec vocem eius aliquando audistis; ideo dicit, quia non obtemperaverunt isti duntaxat cum quibus loquebatur. Quibus dicit etiam: Nec faciem eius vidistis; quia non potest. Quod autem dicit: Neque verbum eius habetis in vobis manens; quia in quo manet verbum Dei, Christus in illo manet, quem isti respuerunt. Nam cum ipse Dominus dixisset: Pater, clarifica me ea claritate qua fui apud te, priusquam mundus fieret; sonuit vox de coelo: Et clarificavi, et clarificabo. Quam vocem multi Iudaeorum praesentes audierunt, nec ideo tamen audisse dicendi sunt, quia non obtemperaverunt ut crederent. Quapropter si non est mirandum quod Verbum Dei, id est, unicus Filius Dei, qui de Patre annuntiat, cui vult per se ipsum, cui vult per aliquam creaturam manifestatur vel sonando, vel apparendo, cum tamen ipse per se ipsum mundo corde videatur, et per illum Pater: Beati enim mundicordes, quia ipsi Deum videbunt, non est mirandum, ex utroque Testamento ista omnia testimonia consonare.

Manichaeis nos parem quaestionem referimus, et quod de Novo Testamento protulerunt, de Veteri Testamento proferimus.

10. De eo quod scriptum est, quod locutus est Deus Moysi et dixit illi: Loquere ad filios Israel: Sumite primitias ab omni homine, quod mihi destinetis, hoc est, aurum, argentum, aeramentum, purpuram, byssum, coccum, pilos caprinos, pelles rubras agnorum, ligna integra, oleum ad illuminationem, thymiamata, lapides pretiosos, hoc est, beryllos; et constituite tabernaculum, in quo commorari vobiscum possim. Commovent etiam hinc Manichaei quaestionem, et huic Scripturarum loco illud in Evangelio dicunt esse contrarium, quod ait Dominus: Non iurabis, neque per coelum, quia sedes Dei est; neque per terram, quia scabellum pedum eius est. Disputant enim, et magnum aliquid sibi videntur dicere, cum dicunt: Quomodo ille Deus, cuius coelum sedes, et terra scabellum pedum eius est, in tabernaculo habitat, quod ex auro, et argento, et aere, et purpura, et pilis pecorum, pellibusque constructum est? Adhibentes etiam testem apostolum Paulum, quia dicit Deum lucem habitare inaccessibilem. Quibus nos parem quaestionem referimus, et quod de Novo Testamento protulerunt, de Veteri Testamento proferimus. Ibi enim invenitur prius scriptum: Coelum mihi sedes est, terra autem scabellum pedum meorum: quam domum aedificabitis mihi, aut quis locus requiei meae? Nonne manus mea fecit haec omnia? Ecce habent ubi libri Veteris Testamenti praedicant Deum in templis manufactis non habitare: et tamen Filius Dei nostri, flagello de restibus facto, expulit de templo eos qui boves et columbas vendebant, et nummulariorum evertit mensas; et ait: Domus Patris mei domus orationis vocabitur, vos autem fecistis illam speluncam latronum. Si ergo aliquis istis duobus ex adverso capitulis constitutis, velit imperitos decipere, et dicere in Veteri Testamento magnificari Deum, cuius dicitur sedes coelum, et terra scabellum pedum, et negatur habitare in domo manufacta; in Novo autem Testamento domus eius dicitur templum constructum ab hominibus: nonne Manichaei vel sero fatebuntur, et habitaculum Dei per manus hominum factum, ad aliquam significationem in utroque Testamento accipi; et Deum non habitare in locis ab hominibus fabricatis, in utroque Testamento praedicari?

Non contraria dicimus esse zelantem Deum, et iustum Deum.

11. De eo quod in Exodo scriptum est: Ne adoraveritis deos alienos; et iterum: Deus vester zelans appellatur; zelans enim zelavit. Huic capitulo quod scriptum est: Ne adoraveritis deos alienos, cum calumniantur Manichaei, satis ostendunt

placere sibi adorari multos deos. Nec mirum, quandoquidem in secta sua numerosissimam deorum familiam commemorant atque commendant: quippe qui etiam ad ista visibilia venerunt, quae pro ipsius veritatis luce venerantur et adorant; et ideo displicet eis quod scriptum est in Exodo: Ne adoraveritis deos alienos. Addunt etiam illud propter hoc dictum esse: Deus vester zelans appellatur; zelans enim zelavit: ut tamquam Deum zelantem non amemus, cuius zelo deos alienos zelare non sinimur. Et ideo dicunt ista Evangelio esse contraria, quoniam Dominus dicit: Pater iuste, et mundus te non cognovit; quasi non sit dicendus Deus iustus, nisi nos deos alienos adorare permittat. Iustum enim Deum et zelantem Deum tamquam contraria sibi esse dissertant, et decipiunt miseros, non intellegentes totam spem salutis nostrae esse zelum Dei. Hoc enim nomine illa eius significatur providentia, qua nullam a se animam fornicari impune permittit, sicut Propheta dicit: Perdes omnes qui fornicantur abs te. Sicut enim ea quae dicitur ira Dei, non perturbatio mentis est, sed potentia vindicandi: sic zelum Dei non cruciatum animi, quo maritus adversus uxorem, vel uxor adversus maritum torqueri solent, sed tranquillissimam sinceriCssimamque iustitiam, qua nulla anima beata esse sinitur, falsis opinionibus pravisque cupiditatibus corrupta, et quodam modo gravidata. Illi enim haec verba horrescunt, qui nondum viderunt ineffabili maiestati Dei nulla verba congruere. Sic enim ab istis verbis temperandum putant, quasi aliquid dignum Deo dicant, cum ista non dicunt. Sanctus enim Spiritus hoc ipsum hominibus intellegentibus insinuans, quam sint ineffabilia summa divina, his etiam verbis uti voluit, quae apud homines in vitio poni solent; ut inde admonerentur, etiam illa quae cum aliqua dignitate Dei se putant homines dicere, indigna esse illius maiestate, cui honorificum potius silentium, quam ulla vox humana competeret. Quaero zelum hominis, et invenio perturbationem cruciantem cor. Tamen cum quaero causam, nihil aliud invenio, nisi quod non patitur coniugis adulterium. Maxime enim et proprie inter coniugia zelotypia dici solet. Itaque si maritus esset per se ipsum beatus et omnipotens et iustus, sine ullo cruciatu, et tota facilitate, et nulla iniquitate peccatum coniugis vindicaret. Quam tamen eius actionem humano loquendi modo etiamsi non proprie, translate tamen et recte zelum vocarem. Quis enim Tullio calumniatus est, qui certe noverat latine loqui, cum ait Caesari: Nulla de virtutibus tuis, nec admirabilior, nec gratior misericordia est? Et tamen ex eo appellatam misericordiam dicunt, quod miserum cor faciat dolentis aliena miseria. Numquid ergo virtus miserum cor facit? Quid ergo calumniosis Tullius responderet, nisi misericordiae nomine clementiam se appellare voluisse? Quoniam recte solemus loqui, non solum verba propria, sed etiam vicina usurpantes. Cuius auctoris mentionem facere volui, quoniam non de re quaestio hic, sed de verbo est. Sicut enim nostri auctores, divinarum scilicet Litterarum, de rebus maxime cogitaverunt; sic mundanorum auctorum prope omnis cura de verbis est. Sed habeo Evangelium, et omnes Novi Testamenti libros, in quibus misericordia Dei frequentissime commendatur. Si audent ergo isti miseri, etiam inde faciant quaestionem, et negent esse misericordem Deum, ne miserum cor habere intellegatur. Sicut ergo potest esse in Deo misericordia sine cordis miseria: sic etiam sine tabe atque cruciatu animi zelum Dei non dedignemur accipere; et humani conditionem sermonis feramus, ut ad divinum perveniamus silentium. Sed si contraria dicunt esse zelantem Deum, et iustum Deum; quid dicturi sunt, cum et in Novo Testamento invenio: Zelo Dei vos zelo; vel adhibitum etiam de veteribus in Evangelio testimonium: Zelus domus tuae comedit me? Rursus in Vetere cum legunt: Iustus Dominus, et iustitias dilexit, aequitatem vidit vultus eius; nonne fatebuntur etiam hoc modo imperitis duo Testamenta videri posse contraria, ut in Novo inveniamus zelum Dei, in Vetere iustitiam Dei? bene autem intellegentibus utrumque in utroque magna sancti Spiritus unitate et pace concinere?

Hinc apparet quia caro et sanguis regnum Dei non possidebunt, quia cum induerit incorruptionem et immortalitatem, iam non caro et sanguis erit, sed in corpus coeleste mutabitur.

12. 1. De eo quod scriptum est, non esse manducandum sanguinem, quod anima sit carnis sanguis. Huic sententiae veteris Legis Manichaei ex Evangelio illud opponunt quod Dominus dicit, non esse timendos eos qui occidere possunt corpus, animae autem nocere non possunt; et disputant dicentes: Si sanguis anima est, quomodo homines potestatem in eam non habent, cum de sanguine multa faciant, sive excipientes et canibus volucribusque in escam proponentes, sive effundentes, aut coeno lutoque miscentes? Haec enim et alia innumerabilia sine difficultate homines de sanguine possunt facere. Ideo isti quaerunt insultantes, quomodo, si sanguis est anima, non possit hominis interfector nocere animae, cum tantam in eius sanguinem habeat potestatem. Addunt etiam quod ait apostolus Paulus: Quia caro et sanguis regnum Dei non possidebunt: et dicunt: Si sanguis est anima, sicut Moyses dicit, nulla invenietur

anima posse regnum Dei adipisci. Cui calumniae primo ita respondendum est, ut ipsi cogantur ostendere ubi scriptum sit in libris veteris Legis, quod anima humana sanguis sit. Nusquam enim hoc invenient in illa Scriptura, quam lacerare miseri quamdiu conantur, nullo modo permittuntur intellegere. Quod si de anima humana nihil tale ibi dictum est, quid ad nos pertinet, si anima pecoris aut laedi ab interfectore potest, aut possidere Dei regnum non potest? Sed quia de animis pecorum nimis sunt isti solliciti (cum enim sint hominum animae rationales, revolvi tamen eas in pecora existimant), clausa sibi esse arbitrantur regna coelorum, si pecorum animis clausa esse consentiant.

12. 2. Quid, quod etiam insultare ausus est populo Israel Adimantus unus ex discipulis Manichaei, quem magnum doctorem illius sectae fuisse commemorant? Insultare ergo ausus est populo Iudaeorum, quod secundum eorum intellectum, quo existimant sanguinem esse animam, parentum ipsorum animae, partim a serpentibus devoratae, partim igne consumptae, partim in desertis atque asperrimis montium locis arefactae sunt. Quod si verum esse quisquam concederet, sine scelere tamen eorum quibus iste insultare voluit, factum esse convinceret. Non enim parentum suorum animas, quibus illa omnia secundum horum intellectum accidisse dixit, ipsi aliqua ex parte laeserunt: quapropter luctum inde possunt habere, non reatum. Quid autem ipse Adimantus faciet secundum opinionem suam, qua credidit etiam rationales, id est, hominum animas in belluina corpora posse contrudi? Quid ergo faciet de tanto scelere, si quando tardum iumentum plagis, aut concitatum freno fatigavit, in quo forte patris eius anima fuerit? ut non dicam quod etiam occidere parentes suos inter pediculos et pulices potuerit, a quorum isti interfectione non temperant. Quid enim eis prodest, quod aliquando negant usque ad ista minutissima animantia revolvi animas humanas posse? Hoc enim negant, ne tam multarum interfectionum rei teneantur, aut cogantur parcere pediculis et pulicibus et cimicibus, et tantas ab eis molestias sine ulla caedis eorum licentia sustinere. Nam vehementer urgentur, cur in vulpeculam revolvi anima humana possit, et non possit in mustelam; cum catulus vulpeculae fortasse etiam minor sit, quam magna mustela. Deinde si in mustelam potest, cur in murem non potest? Et si in istum potest, cur in stellionem non potest? Et si in eum potest, cur in locustam non potest? Deinde in apem, deinde in muscam, deinde in cimicem, atque inde usque in pulicem, et si quid est aliud multo minutius, pervenire? Ubi enim terminum constituant, non inveniunt:

atque ita per istam nugatoriam credulitatem, conscientiae illorum innumerabilibus homicidiorum sceleribus obruuntur.

12. 3. Nam ex eo quod scriptum est, sanguinem pecoris animam eius esse; praeter id quod supra dixi, non ad me pertinere quid agatur de pecoris anima; possum etiam interpretari praeceptum illud in signo esse positum. Non enim Dominus dubitavit dicere: Hoc est corpus meum; cum signum daret corporis sui.

12. 4. Quod autem ait Apostolus: Caro et sanguis regnum Dei non possidebunt; etiam in Lege dictum est: Non permanebit in istis spiritus meus, quoniam caro sunt. Et toties in veteribus Libris iustorum animis praemium futurum promittitur. Sed tamen Apostolus volens insinuare quale corpus iustorum per immutationem in resurrectione futurum sit, quia non nubent, neque uxores ducent, sed erunt sicut Angeli in coelis; hanc ergo immutationem futuram corporum sanctorum volens insinuare, dixit Apostolus: Dico enim vobis, fratres, quia caro et sanguis regnum Dei non possidebunt. Quod non una separata et ad fraudem commemorata sententia, sed toto ipso Epistolae loco pertractato, vel potius lecto (non enim res obscura est) inveniri potest. Sic enim dicit: Oportet corruptibile hoc induere incorruptionem, et mortale hoc induere immortalitatem. Quod eum de corpore dicere, de superioribus manifeste invenitur, cum ait: Non omnis caro eadem caro: alia quidem hominum, alia autem pecorum; alia caro volucrum, alia piscium. Et corpora coelestia, et corpora terrestria: sed alia est coelestium gloria, alia terrestrium; alia gloria solis, alia gloria lunae, et alia gloria stellarum. Stella enim ab stella differt in gloria; sic et resurrectio mortuorum. Seminatur in corruptione, surget in incorruptione: seminatur in contumelia, surget in gloria: seminatur in infirmitate, surget in virtute: seminatur corpus animale, surget corpus spiritale. Si est corpus animale, est et spiritale, sicut scriptum est: Factus est primus homo Adam in animam viventem, novissimus Adam in spiritum vivificantem. Sed non primum quod spiritale est, sed quod animale; postea, quod spiritale. Primus homo de terra, terrenus; secundus homo de coelo, coelestis. Qualis terrenus, tales et terreni; et qualis coelestis, tales et coelestes. Et quomodo induimus imaginem terreni, induamus et imaginem eius qui de coelo est. Hoc autem dico, fratres, quia caro et sanguis regnum Dei haereditate possidere non possunt; neque corruptio incorruptionem haereditate possidebit. Certe iam

clarum est quare hoc Apostolus dixerit. Quid ergo iste tam turpi fraude non commemorat, nisi hoc ultimum, et tacet illa superiora, quibus hoc quod male interpretatur, bene possit intellegi? Nam quoniam Domini nostri corpus post resurrectionem sic levatum est in coelum, ut pro ipsa coelesti habitatione coelestem acceperit mutationem, et hoc sperare in die ultimo iussi sumus; ideo dixit Apostolus: Qualis terrenus, tales et terreni, id est, mortales; et qualis coelestis, tales et coelestes, id est, immortales, non solum animis, sed etiam corporibus. Unde et supra dixerat, aliam esse coelestium corporum gloriam, et aliam terrestrium. Quod autem spiritale dixit corpus in resurrectione futurum, non propterea putandum est, quod non corpus, sed spiritus erit: sed spiritale corpus omni modo spiritui subditum dicit, sine aliqua corruptione vel morte. Non enim quia quod modo habemus corpus animale appellat, ideo putandum est non illud esse corpus, sed animam. Ergo quemadmodum corpus animale nunc dicitur, quia subditum est animae; spiritale autem nondum dici potest, quia nondum spiritui plene subiectum est, quamdiu corrumpi potest: sic et tunc spiritale vocabitur, cum spiritui atque aeternitati nulla corruptione resistere poterit.

12. 5. Aut si adhuc parum videtur esse monstratum, quod sententiam istam propter immutationem quae futura est Apostolus dixerit, cum ait: Caro et sanguis regnum Dei haereditate possidere non possunt, neque corruptio incorruptionem haereditate possidebit; attendite quid continuo subiciat, et adiungat: Ecce mysterium vobis dico: omnes quidem resurgemus, non tamen omnes immutabimur, in atomo, in ictu oculi, in novissima tuba. Canet enim tuba, et mortui resurgent incorrupti, et nos immutabimur. Deinde contexit, et dicit etiam illud quod paulo ante commemoravi, ut ostendat qualis futura sit ipsa immutatio. Statim quippe dicit: Oportet enim corruptibile hoc induere incorruptionem, et mortale hoc induere immortalitatem. Hinc ergo apparet quia caro et sanguis regnum Dei non possidebunt, quia cum induerit incorruptionem et immortalitatem, iam non caro et sanguis erit, sed in corpus coeleste mutabitur. Quod quidem ex occasione tractavimus, quia huic quoque sententiae multum insidiari solent, negantes corporum resurrectionem. Nam ista quaestio non de corpore, sed de anima proposita est, quam putant sic accipi in Lege, ut sanguis esse existimetur: quod nos nullo modo sic intellegimus. Sed quamvis de pecorum animis non curemus, cum quibus non habemus rationis aliquam societatem: tamen illud quod Lex dixit, fundendum esse sanguinem,

nec in escam assumendum, quia sanguis est anima, in signo esse positum dicimus sicut alia multa; et pene omnia Scripturarum illarum sacramenta signis et figuris plena sunt futurae praedicationis, quae iam per Dominum nostrum Iesum Christum declarata est. Sic est enim sanguis anima, quomodo petra erat Christus, sicut dicit Apostolus: Bibebant enim de spiritali sequente petra, petra autem erat Christus. Notum est autem filios Israel petra percussa bibisse aquam in eremo, de quibus loquebatur Apostolus, cum haec diceret; nec tamen ait: Petra significabat Christum; sed ait: Petra erat Christus. Quae rursus ne carnaliter acciperetur, spiritalem illam vocat; id est, eam spiritaliter intellegi docet. Longum est, et nunc non necessarium, sacramenta eiusdem Legis exponere, nisi cum breviter possint. Sufficit autem ut noverint illi qui de his calumniantur, non ea nos ita intellegere, ut illa solent irridere; sed quemadmodum Apostoli omnia intellegentes pauca exposuerunt, ut ad easdem regulas cetera posteris intellegenda relinquerent.

Adimanti calumnias refutandas refellendasque suscepimus.

13. 1. De eo quod scriptum est in Deuteronomio: Videte ne obliviscamini testamentum Dei vestri quod conscripsit, et faciatis vobis effigies et imagines; addidit etiam dicens: Deus vester ignis est edax, et Deus zelans. Haec verba de Scripturis hoc modo ille Adimantus proposuit. Eius enim calumnias refutandas refellendasque suscepimus. Sed et iam superius de zelo Dei cum calumniaretur, puto satis esse responsum. Meminerimus tamen non solum ibi, sed etiam hic, sic eum de zelo Dei criminatum Scripturas, ut adiungeret etiam quod de simulacris non colendis in illis libris praecipitur a Domino Deo nostro; quasi non ob aliud reprehendat zelum Dei, nisi quod illo ipso zelo a cultu simulacrorum prohibemur: vult ergo videri favere se simulacris. Quod propterea faciunt, ut miserrimae et vesanae suae sectae etiam Paganorum concilient benevolentiam. Huic autem Legis capitulo etiam illud opponunt, ubi quidam accessit ad Dominum, et ait illi: Magister bone, quid faciens vitam aeternam possidebo? Cui respondit Iesus: Quid me interrogas de bono? Nemo bonus, nisi unus Deus. Ut ex hoc videlicet contraria ista esse arbitremur, quia in Lege dicitur: Deus ignis edax, et: Deus zelans; in Evangelio autem: Nemo bonus, nisi unus Deus.

13. 2. Et de zelo quidem iam responsum est, non sic esse ista verba in Scripturis posita, ut aliquam Dei perturbationem cruciatumve significent: sed quia nihil dignum de Deo dici potest, propterea usque ad ista perventum est, quae cum homines indigna esse putaverint, cogantur discere, etiam illa quae convenienter de ineffabili divina excellentia se dicere existimant, indigna esse maiestate Dei; cuius sapientia cum descensura esset usque ad corpus humanum, prius usque ad humana verba descendit. Ecce dixi, descendit: quod verbum si discutere coepero, proprie me dixisse non video; non enim potest descendere, nisi quod etiam de loco in locum moveri potest. Nam qui descendit, locum superiorem deserere, et inferiorem petere videtur. Dei autem Sapientia, cum tota ubique praesto sit, nullo pacto migrare de loco in locum potest. De qua Ioannes in Evangelio melius ait, tamquam dominici pectoris particeps. Ait enim: In hoc mundo erat, et mundus per ipsum factus est, et mundus eum non cognovit; et tamen ipse adiungit et dicit: In sua propria venit, et sui eum non receperunt. Quomodo hic erat, et quomodo venit, nisi quia illa sublimitas ineffabilis, ut hominibus congruat, humanis sonis significanda est; ut autem deos homines faciat, divino est intellegenda silentio? Potest ergo reddi ratio, quare ita dictum sit; non tamen potest aliquid de Deo digne dici, quod ideo iam indignum est, quia potuit dici. Tolle de zelo errorem et dolorem, quid remanebit aliud, nisi voluntas custodiens castitatem, et corruptionem vindicans coniugalem? Quo igitur verbo, nisi zelo Dei melius posset insinuari, quod vocamur ad coniugium Dei, et non vult nos turpi amore corrumpi, et punit impudicitiam nostram, et diligit castitatem? Non enim frustra vulgo dici solet: Qui non zelat, non amat.

13. 3. Ad hoc etiam pertinet quod dictum est: edax ignis; de quo disputare non debeo, sed potius ipsos interrogare, quem ignem dixerit Dominus se venisse mittere in hunc mundum. Hoc enim dictum est in Evangelio, quod illi accusare non possunt, non ut Christum honorent, sed ut decipiant Christianos. Quod cum eis commemoratum fuerit, quemadmodum Dominus dixerit: Ignem veni mittere in hunc mundum; miseri dicunt: Sed illud aliud est. Quibus respondemus: Et hoc aliud est, noli metuere. Nam ipse Christus loquitur etiam in Veteri Testamento, cum dicit: Ego sum ignis edax; qui loquitur in Evangelio, quod ignem venerit in hunc mundum mittere, id est, Verbum Dei, quod est ipse. Nam veteres utique Scripturas exposuit post resurrectionem discipulis, incipiens a Moyse et Prophetis omnibus, quando ipsi discipuli ignem se accepisse confessi sunt, dicentes: Nonne cor nostrum ardens erat in nobis in

via, cum aperiret nobis Scripturas? Ipse est ignis edax: consumit enim veterem vitam divinus amor, et innovat hominem: ut ex eo quod Deus ignis est edax, faciat ut eum nos amemus; ex eo autem quod Deus zelans est, ipse nos amet. Nolite ergo timere ignem, quod est Deus: sed timete ignem, quem paravit haereticis Deus.

13. 4. Quod enim Adimantus elegit de Evangelio locum, quem huic Legis capitulo tamquam contrarium apud imperitos obiceret, ubi ait Dominus: Nemo bonus, nisi unus Deus, quoties invenitur bonitas Dei in Veteri Testamento, quis numerare sufficiat? Unum tamen ponam, quod quotidie in Ecclesia cantatur: Confitemini Domino, quoniam bonus, quoniam in saeculum misericordia eius. Certe et hoc zelanti Deo, sicut Manichaei existimant, videtur esse contrarium, et tamen in libris Veteris Testamenti cantatur. Item rex ille, qui cum filio suo nuptias faceret, invenit inter discumbentes hominem non habentem vestem nuptialem; et eum primo amici nomine appellans, manibus et pedibus colligatis mitti iussit in tenebras exteriores: moleste intellegentibus non videtur bonus. Et si ipsum quisquam capitulum Evangelii proponeret, et sicut facit Adimantus de Veteri Testamento, ita Evangelium calumniose accusaret, laudans potius Veteris Testamenti libros, ubi scriptum est: Confitemini Domino, quoniam bonus, quoniam in saeculum misericordia eius; et reprehendens in Novo, quod vocatus conviva in tantum supplicium propter vestem mittitur; et hoc fraudulenta perversitate assidue faceret, ut omnia loca lenitatis de Veteri Testamento colligeret, et loca severitatis de Novo, et haec sibi adversa esse contenderet, laudans Vetus, et reprehendens Novum: similiter inveniret imperitos et divinarum Scripturarum miserabiliter ignaros, quibus persuaderet Vetus potius Testamentum, quam Novum esse retinendum. Quod cum isti ex alia parte faciunt, id est, Vetus reprehendentes, quasi contrarium Novo, miror quod non cogitant posse aliquem aliquando utrumque legere, et divina ope intellectum utrumque laudare; fraudemque istorum atque malitiam vel dolere tamquam hominum, vel cavere tamquam haereticorum, vel irridere tamquam imperitorum et superborum.

Quod omnia munda sint mundis, servata moderatione evangelica.

14. 1. De eo quod scriptum est in Deuteronomio: Secundum desiderium animae tuae occide, et manduca omnem carnem, iuxta voluptatem quam dedit tibi Dominus. Cave autem ne sanguinem manduces; sed effunde tamquam aquam super terram. His verbis Legis Adimantus contrarium esse arbitratur quod in Evangelio Dominus ait: Ne graventur corda vestra cruditate, et vinolentia, et curis saecularibus; et quod ait Apostolus: Bonum est non manducare carnem, neque bibere vinum; et iterum: Non potestis mensae Domini communicare, et mensae daemoniorum. Nos autem omnia haec, sive quae in Veteri, sive quae in Novo Testamento scripta sunt, et suis causis exigentibus posita dicimus, et sibi adversa non esse monstramus. Quamquam et ipse in his verbis quae posuit de Veteri Testamento, animadvertere potuit, non ad immoderatam voracitatem pertinere quod dictum est: Secundum desiderium animae tuae occide, et manduca omnem carnem; quando sequitur, iuxta voluptatem quam dedit tibi Dominus. Immoderatam enim voluptatem non dedit tibi Dominus, sed quanta sustentationi naturae salutique sufficiat. Quisquis autem sequitur immoderatam voracitatem, suum vitium sequitur, non eam voluptatem quam dedit Dominus: et ideo non est contrarium quod in Evangelio positum est: Non graventur corda vestra cruditate, et vinolentia, et curis saecularibus. Cum enim quisque non replet nisi eam voluptatem quam Dominus dedit, id est, modestam atque naturalem, non gravatur cor eius cruditate, et vinolentia, et curis saecularibus.

14. 2. De carne autem non manducanda et non bibendo vino quod ait Apostolus, non quia illa immunda arbitratus est, hoc praecepit, sicut isti exstimant, et errantes in errorem praecipitant, quibus talia persuaserunt: sed cum ipse posuerit causam cur hoc dixerit, non est nobis haec interpretanda vel exponenda sententia. Sufficit enim ipsum de Apostoli Epistola totum locum huic sermoni contexere, ut et causa manifeste appareat cur hoc Apostolus dixerit; et istorum fraus, qui particulas quasdam de Scripturis eligunt, quibus decipiant imperitos, non connectentes quae supra et infra scripta sunt, ex quibus voluntas et intentio scriptoris possit intellegi. Sic ergo Apostolus ait: Infirmum autem in fide recipite, non in diiudicationibus cogitationum. Alius quidem credit manducare omnia: qui autem infirmus est, olera manducet. Qui manducat, non manducantem non spernat; et qui non manducat, manducantem non iudicet: Deus enim illum recepit. Tu quis es, qui iudices alienum servum? Suo domino stat, aut cadit. Stabit autem: potens est enim

Dominus statuere illum. Alius quidem iudicat alternos dies, alius autem iudicat omnem diem. Unusquisque in suo sensu abundet. Qui sapit diem, Domino sapit: et qui manducat, Domino manducat; gratias enim agit Deo: et qui non manducat, Domino non manducat, et gratias agit Deo. Nemo enim nostrum sibi vivit, et nemo sibi moritur. Sive enim vivimus, Domino vivimus; sive morimur, Domino morimur. Sive ergo vivimus, sive morimur, Domini sumus. Ad hoc enim Christus mortuus est et resurrexit, ut mortuorum et vivorum dominetur. Tu autem, quare iudicas fratrem tuum? aut tu quare spernis fratrem tuum? Omnes enim stabimus ante tribunal Domini. Scriptum est enim: Vivo ego, dicit Dominus, quia mihi curvabit omne genu, et confitebitur omnis lingua Deo. Igitur unusquisque nostrum pro se rationem reddet. Non ergo amplius invicem iudicemus: sed hoc magis iudicate, ne ponatis offendiculum aut scandalum fratribus. Scio et certus sum in Domino Iesu, quia nihil commune per illum, nisi ei qui putat aliquid esse commune, illi commune est. Nam si propter escam frater tuus contristatur, iam non secundum caritatem ambulas. Noli in esca tua illum perdere, pro quo Christus mortuus est. Non ergo blasphemetur bonum nostrum. Non est enim regnum Dei esca et potus; sed iustitia, et pax, et gaudium in Spiritu sancto. Qui enim in hoc servit Christo, placet Deo, et probatus est hominibus. Itaque quae pacis sunt sectemur, et quae ad aedificationem sunt in invicem. Noli propter escam destruere opus Dei. Omnia quidem munda, sed malum est homini qui per offensionem manducat. Bonum est non manducare carnem, neque bibere vinum, neque in quo frater tuus offenditur. Tu fidem quam habes penes temetipsum, habe coram Deo. Beatus qui non iudicat semetipsum in quo probat. Qui autem discernit, si manducaverit, damnatus est, quia non ex fide. Omne autem quod non est ex fide, peccatum est. Numquid eget cuiusquam interpretatione, ut intellegatur cur hoc Apostolus dixerit; et quanta illi malitia de Scripturis certa quaeque discerpunt, quibus circumveniant imperitos? Nam et munda esse omnia dixit Apostolus secundum fidem; et ei esse immunda, qui putat immunda: et tunc esse ab eis temperandum, cum per offensionem accipiuntur, id est, cum aliquis infirmus putat sibi ab omnibus carnibus temperandum, ne incidat in carnem immolatitiam; et ideo eum qui manducat, potest arbitrari in honorem idolorum id facere, et ex eo graviter offendi: cum ipsa immolatitia caro, si ex fide a nesciente accipiatur, neminem maculet. Unde alio loco idem apostolus interrogari vetat, cum quid de macello emitur, vel ab aliquo infideli quisquam vocatus, in mensa eius exhiberi sibi carnes videt, quas isti immundas arbitrantur, non propter immolationem, sed quia carnes sunt, cum Apostolus clamet omnia munda esse, et omnem creaturam Dei bonam esse, et omnia sanctificari per verbum et orationem: et tamen temperandum ab eis, si quis forte infirmus offenditur. Et quodam loco apertissime istos significavit, cum dicit, in novissimis temporibus futuros quosdam prohibentes nubere, abstinentes a cibis quos Deus creavit. Hos enim proprie designat, qui non propterea temperant a cibis talibus, ut aut concupiscentiam suam refrenent, aut infirmitati alterius parcant, sed quia ipsas carnes immundas putant, et earum creatorem Deum esse negant. Nos autem teneamus apostolicam disciplinam dicentem, quod omnia munda sint mundis, servata moderatione evangelica, ut non graventur corda nostra cruditate, et vinolentia, et curis saecularibus.

14. 3. Nam idem illud quod Apostolus ait: Non potestis mensae Domini communicare, et mensae daemoniorum; non video cur opponendum huic loco Legis, et quasi contrarium Manichaei esse crediderint. Non enim de immolationibus Lex loquitur, cum in Deuteronomio dicitur: Secundum desiderium animae tuae occide, et manduca omnem carnem, iuxta voluptatem quam dedit tibi Dominus; sed de cibis qui pertinent ad hominis alimentum. Sed quoniam Manichaei etiam cum ad hominis coenam quaeque animalia praeparantur, immolationem esse dicunt; secundum suum intellectum ista contraria esse putaverunt. Propterea et illum commemoraverunt locum, ubi Apostolus ait: Quae immolant Gentes, daemoniis immolant, et non Deo; cum Apostolus apertissime de victimis loqueretur, quae in templo offeruntur daemonibus; non de his escis quas sibi homines praeparant. Sic enim dicit: Quid ergo? dico quia idolis immolatum est aliquid, aut idolum est aliquid? Sed quia quae immolant, daemoniis, et non Deo immolant. Nolo vos socios daemoniorum fieri. Non potestis calicem Domini bibere, et calicem daemoniorum. Non potestis mensae Domini participare, et mensae daemoniorum. An aemulamur Dominum? Numquid fortiores illo sumus? Omnia licita sunt, sed non omnia expediunt: omnia licita sunt, sed non omnia aedificant. Nemo quod suum est quaerat, sed id quod alterius. Omne quod in macello venit, manducate, nihil interrogantes propter conscientiam. Domini enim est terra et plenitudo eius. Si quis vos vocaverit ex infidelibus, et volueritis ire; omnia quae apponuntur vobis, manducate, nihil diiudicantes propter conscientiam. Si quis autem vobis dixerit quia hoc immolatitium est, nolite manducare, propter illum qui indicavit, et propter conscientiam: conscientiam

autem dico, non tuam, sed alterius. Quare enim libertas mea iudicatur ab alia conscientia? Si ego cum gratia participo, utquid blasphemor, pro quo ego gratias ago? Sive igitur manducatis, sive bibitis, sive quodcumque facitis, omnia in gloriam Dei facite. Haec attendant Manichaei, et videant quomodo dictum sit in Deuteronomio: Secundum desiderium animae tuae occide, et manduca omnem carnem, iuxta voluptatem quam Dominus dedit tibi. Quod enim de quibusdam carnibus non manducandis Iudaeis praeceptum est, et immundae sunt dictae, ad significationem valet hominum immundorum, qui per figuras in veteribus Scripturis sunt designati. Sicuti enim bos ille, cui trituranti vetat os alligari, evangelistam significat, sicut Apostolus apertissime exponit; sic et illa quae prohibita sunt, quasdam hominum immunditias significant, quae in societatem corporis Christi, id est, in Ecclesiam stabilem et sempiternam non recipiuntur. Nam quod ad cibos attinet, omnino nihil immundum esse, sed malum esse homini qui per offensionem manducat, manifestissime apparet. Adimantus tamquam sibi adversa atque contraria de utroque Testamento capitula obiecit.

15. 1. De eo quod in Levitico scriptum est: Separate a mundo immundum, et nemo manducet carnem cameli, asini, et leporis, et porci, et aquilae, et milvi, et corvi, et vulturis, et reliquorum. Nusquam manifestius plenissima dolis et fraudibus anima huius hominis deprehendi potest, qui tamquam sibi adversa atque contraria de utroque Testamento capitula obiecit, quam in hoc loco ubi commemoravit in Levitico scriptum esse, ut a nonnullis animalium carnibus temperetur. Namque huic sententiae illud ex Evangelio credidit opponendum, ubi Dominus dicit: Nihil est ingrediens in hominem, coinquinans eum; sed ea quae procedunt de eo, coinquinant. Hoc si imprudens fecit, nihil caecius: si autem sciens, nihil sceleratius. Nonne ipse paulo ante posuerat Apostoli testimonium dicentis: Bonum est, fratres, non manducare carnem, neque bibere vinum; dum cupit de Novo Testamento Veteri adversari, ubi dictum est: Secundum desiderium animae tuae occide, et manduca omnem carnem? Quomodo ergo nunc placet ei sententia Domini, qua dicit, nihil esse ingrediens in hominem quod coinquinet eum, sed ea coinquinare quae de homine procedunt? Ubi se iste abscondat ab hac sententia? Quo fugiet, dicat mihi, quando immunditiam carnium fugiendam et a cibis sanctorum separandam, perversa et superstitiosa imaginatione continentiae praecipit? Certe enim, si verum est, non coinquinare illa quae ingrediuntur in hominem, cum magno

errore immundas esse dicunt escas Manichaei, cum homines carne vescuntur. Si autem immundae sunt tales escae, quid de isto testimonio facient, quod evangelica et divina auctoritate prolatum est, ubi Dominus dicit, non coinquinari hominem iis quae ingrediuntur in eum, sed iis quae procedunt de illo? An forte dicturi sunt, sicut solent dicere, cum Scripturarum eos urget auctoritas, hoc capitulum a corruptoribus Scripturarum insertum esse Evangelio? Cur ergo Adimantus hoc capitulo teste utitur, et inde conatur Vetus Testamentum oppugnare, unde iste prosternitur? Cum enim quispiam catholicus christianus utriusque Scripturae venerator et intellector ei responderit, haec non esse contraria; quod illa de quorumdam carnibus animalium, quibus non esse vescendum populo adhuc carnali praeceptum est, ad significationem posita sint humanorum morum, quos Ecclesia quae corpus est Domini, in suae unitatis vinculum stabile et sempiternum recipere non potest, tamquam immundas escas respuens, et in sua viscera non convertens; ut omnia illa praecepta carnali populo imposita futuram disciplinam spiritalis populi prophetarent: et ideo non ea repugnare sententiae Domini, qua verissime dicit, non coinquinari hominem iis quae per escam ingrediuntur in eum. Illa enim sententia servis onera imponit; ista iam liberis iugum excutit servitutis. Et illa tamen sic dicta est, ut servorum onera fidem praenuntient liberorum. Omnia enim, sicut dicit Apostolus, in figura contingebant illis; scripta sunt autem propter nos, in quos finis saeculorum obvenit. Si ergo in figuram contingebant quae patiebantur, in figuram accipiebant quae monebantur.

15. 2. Cum ergo ista respondero, et hoc modo non esse contraria duo ista capitula de singulis Testamentis collata monstravero, quid iste facturus est, contra quem dicit gravissimum testimonium testis quem contra adversarium ipse produxit? Ipse enim commemoravit de Evangelio testimonium, Domino dicente non coinquinari hominem iis escis quae ingrediuntur in eum: et ipse a carnibus abstinendum tamquam ab immundis escis monere et docere non cessat. Et tamen sensit quantam plagam sibi infligeret, et quanto ictu repercussus se ipse sauciaret. Ne quis enim eum interrogaret et diceret: Quomodo ergo prohibetis carnibus vesci, si Dominus dicit, sicut tu ipse commemoras: Nihil est ingrediens in hominem, coinquinans eum; sed ea quae procedunt de eo, coinquinant? voluit quasi adhibere medicinam sine causa in mortifero vulnere. Sic enim posuit ipsum evangelicum testimonium. In

Evangelio, inquit, dicit ad turbam Dominus: Audite, et intellegite: Nihil est ingrediens in hominem, coinquinans eum, et cetera. Quod ergo commemoravit Dominum hoc ad turbam dixisse, nihil aliud ostendit, nisi non se ignorantia, sed malitia fecisse quod fecit: ut postea diceret Auditoribus suis ad turbam Dominum ista locutum esse, non ad paucos sanctos, quales se ipsi videri volunt; ut quoniam suos Auditores tamquam adhuc immundos permittunt carnibus vesci, sibi autem quasi iam mundis cum sceleratum atque nefarium esse arbitrantur, hoc etiam Dominum sensisse videatur, quod non paucos sanctos, sed turbas ista docuerit. O hominem pessimum, securum de neglegentia generis humani ad occultandas deceptiones suas! Non enim credebat aliquem existere, qui arriperet Evangelium, et cum scientia legeret, et inveniret hominem in ipsis pratis, quibus greges suos Dominus pascit, laqueos incautis et minus providis abscondentem. Nam de his verbis commoti discipuli, et non credentes proprie, sed potius figurate Dominum locutum fuisse, cum diceret non coinquinari hominem iis quae per cibos ingrediuntur in eum, quoniam Iudaei erant etiam ipsi discipuli, qui fugiendos quarumdam carnium cibos a pueritia institutum acceperant, accedentes ad eum dixerunt ei: Scis quia Pharisaei audito verbo scandalizati sunt? At ille respondens ait: Omnis plantatio quam non plantavit Pater meus coelestis, eradicabitur. Sinite illos; caeci sunt, et duces caecorum. Caecus autem si caeco ducatum praestet, ambo in foveam cadunt. Cum ergo infidelitatem Iudaeorum plantationem appellaret quam non plantavit Pater coelestis, tamen adhuc Petrus putans esse illam parabolam, et propterea reprehensos Iudaeos et caecos dictos, quod eam intellegere non potuerint, respondens dixit ei: Edissere nobis parabolam istam. Et ille manifestissime ostendens non esse parabolam, sed propriam locutionem, dixit ad eos: Adhuc et vos sine intellectu estis? Non intellegitis quia omne quod in os intrat, in ventrem vadit, et in secessum emittitur? Quae autem procedunt de ore, de corde exeunt, et ea coinquinant hominem. De corde enim exeunt cogitationes malae, homicidia, adulteria, fornicationes, furta, falsa testimonia, blasphemiae; haec sunt quae coinquinant hominem. Non lotis autem manibus manducare, non coinquinat hominem. De non lotis autem manibus Iudaei moverant quaestionem, cuius occasione Dominus generaliter de iis quae in os intrant, et in ventrem vadunt, et in secessum emittuntur, hoc est, de alimentis nostris dixit sententiam. Quamquam ergo convocatis ad se turbis eum dixisse scriptum sit: Non quod intrat in os coinquinat hominem, sed quod procedit ex ore; tamen iste quo timore hoc addiderit verbis suis, quibus huiusmodi testimonium commemoravit, satis apparet, sicut paulo ante dictum est, ut haberet quod responderet eis qui sibi quaestionem movissent, cur primates Manichaeorum nefas sibi esse existimant carnibus vesci: videlicet ut illud quod Dominus ait, turbis tantum, non Electis concessisse videretur. Sed cum ex consequentibus declaratum sit etiam Petro seorsum interroganti, audientibusque discipulis, quos utique ad culmen Ecclesiae producebat, ita respondisse Dominum, ut neque per parabolam se illa dixisse testatus sit, et ad omnes pertinere monstraverit; non habent isti unde auferant cibos de faucibus hominum, et eas laqueo superstitionis astringant.

15. 3. Fortassis aliquis eorum dicat: Edissere ergo quid significet caro porci, et cameli, et leporis, et milvi, et corvi, et ceterorum, a quibus abstinendum in Lege praecipitur. Nolo, quia longum est. Sed fac me non posse; numquid propterea nullus potest? Et sunt iam volumina innumerabilia in quibus ista exposita sunt. Nobis tamen ad hos refellendos satis est, quod eas observationes umbram esse futurorum, non ego, sed Apostolus dicit, cum etiam vetat serviliter observari, sed tamen aliquid significare declarat, dicens: Nemo ergo vos iudicet in cibo, aut in potu, aut in parte diei festi, aut neomeniae, aut sabbatorum, quod est umbra futurorum. Illa itaque futura quae illis observationibus significabantur, posteaquam per Dominum Iesum Christum venerunt, ablatae sunt serviles observationes: sed earum interpretationes tenentur a liberis. Quidquid enim futuram Ecclesiam significavit, prophetia est. Habes autem eumdem Apostolum dicentem: Spiritum nolite spernere, prophetiam nolite exstinguere; omnia legite, quae bona sunt tenete. Legenda est ergo Scriptura divina, et Spiritus sancti dispensatio cognoscenda, et intuenda prophetia; et reicienda carnalis servitus, et liberalis intellegentia retinenda.

Dominus Legis auctoritatem confirmat, et tamen cavendos et fugiendos esse mores eorum qui Legi non obtemperabant, apertissime ostendit.

16. 1. De eo quod scriptum est in Deuteronomio: Observa et sanctifica diem quem praecepit tibi Dominus. Sex diebus laborabis, et facies omne opus tuum; septima vero die sabbati epulare Domino Deo tuo, nullum faciens opus ipse tu, aut filius tuus, aut filia tua, aut puer tuus, aut puella tua, bos tuus, et asinus tuus, omnia iumenta tua, et colonus tuus. Sic autem quiescet servus tuus et ancilla tua, quemadmodum et tu. Memento quoniam servus fuisti in Aegypto,

et eruit te Dominus Deus tuus in manu potenti et brachio excelso. Idcirco praecepit tibi Dominus custodire diem septimum. Et iterum in Genesi scriptum est quemadmodum Abrahae de circumcisione loquitur: Testamentum meum custodi, inquit, tu et semen tuum, quod erit post te. Hoc est testamentum meum quod servabis inter me, et te et semen tuum: omne masculinum circumcides in carne praeputii ipsorum; et sit hoc signum testamenti inter me et vos. Octava autem die circumcidetis omnes masculos in gente vestra, ut etiam dominatum et comparatum circumcidatis praeter alienigenam: et hoc erit testamentum in gente vestra. Et omnis masculus qui non circumcidet praeputium suum, perdet animam suam de media plebe, quia testamentum meum dissolvit. Haec omnia verba Veteris Testamenti, ut eis de Novo Testamento adversetur, proponit Adimantus, et contraria esse affirmat ea quae Dominus dicit in Evangelio de proselyto: Vae vobis, Scribae et Pharisaei hypocritae, qui circumitis mare et terram ut faciatis unum proselytum; et cum feceritis, erit filius gehennae, multo plus quam estis vos. Quasi vero propterea Dominus proselytum dicat filium gehennae, quia circumciditur, et sabbatum observat; et non potius quia Iudaeorum perditos mores et eorum pravam conversationem cogitur imitari, non qua observant praecepta Legis, sed qua faciunt contra Legem. Quod alio loco de his apertissime dicit, ubi ait quod reiiciunt mandatum Dei, ut suam constitutionem confirment: quia cum Lex praeceperit honorari patrem et matrem, instituerunt ipsi quomodo exhonorentur parentes. Et item cum eis dicit: Vae vobis, Scribae et Pharisaei, qui habetis clavem regni coelorum, nec ipsi intratis, nec alios permittitis intrare. Vel cum alio loco praecepit audientibus, ut dictis Pharisaeorum et Scribarum obtemperarent, facta vero eorum non imitarentur. Ait enim: Super cathedram Moysi sedent: quae dicunt, facite; sed quae faciunt, facere nolite: dicunt enim, et non faciunt. Quo loco et auctoritatem Legis quae per Moysen data est, confirmat Dominus, et tamen cavendos et fugiendos esse mores eorum qui Legi quam acceperant non obtemperabant, apertissime ostendit. Istis autem perversitatibus suis faciebant, ut cum aliquis gentilis ad Legem eorum transisset, id est, factus esset proselytus, haberet mores eorum, et fieret filius gehennae, multo plus quam ipsi essent. Dabant enim magnam operam ut Iudaeus fieret aliquis ex Gentibus, et Iudaeum factum cogebant suos mores pessimos imitari.

Quod non est umbra in corpore figuranda, sed res ipsa in corde gestanda.

16. 2. Neque illud quod de Apostolo tamquam contrarium commemorat, potuit advertere Adimantus manichaeus, omnino non esse contrarium; quia totus eius oculus non ad inquisitionem, sed ad reprehensionem Scripturae intentus erat. Commemorat enim dicentem Apostolum: Circumcisus aliquis vocatus est? non adducat praeputium. In praeputio quis vocatus est? non circumcidatur: quia praeputium nihil est, et circumcisio nihil est, sed observatio praeceptorum Dei. Quid enim manifestius quam hoc Apostolum praecipere, ut unusquisque sicut vocatus erat, sic maneret? Advenientibus enim rebus, quarum erant umbrae illae observationes, id actum est, ut ostenderetur in ipsis umbris non esse spem ponendam, sed in ipsis rebus quas illae umbrae significabant esse venturas, id est, Christum et Ecclesiam. Et propterea illa iam omnia inania erant: nec tamen ea tamquam noxia removenda, sed tamquam superflua contemnenda Apostolus praecipit; ut si quis Iudaeus Christo credidisset, propter offensionem suorum non prohiberetur in ipsis superfluis remanere, nec tamen in eis salutem suam constitutam putaret: non enim signa illa, sed ea quae his significantur in salutem introducunt. Ideoque praeputium nihil est, et circumcisio nihil est, sed observatio mandatorum Dei. Et quod alio loco ait: Utinam et abscindantur qui vos conturbant; non quia circumcisio contraria est Evangelio, dicit Apostolus, sicut Manichaei putant: sed illud est Evangelio contrarium, ut quisque rem deserens, quae per illam umbram figuratur, ipsius umbrae sequatur inanitatem. Quod volebant qui Gentibus in Christum credentibus iugum circumcisionis imponebant quasi ad salutem necessarium, cum iam non esset umbra in corpore figuranda, sed res ipsa in corde gestanda.

Duorum Testamentorum differentiam sic probamus, ut in illo sint onera servorum, in isto gloria liberorum.

16. 3. Et quod dicit: Dies observatis, et sabbata, et solemnitates; timeo vos, ne frustra laboraverim in vobis; non sic scriptum est ut Adimantus ponit. Non enim nominat ibi sabbatum Apostolus. Dicit enim: Dies observatis et annos, et tempora; timeo vos, ne frustra laboraverim in vobis. Sed puta esse de sabbato dictum. Numquid et nos non dicimus ista non esse observanda, sed illa potius quae his significantur? Illi enim ea serviliter observabant, non intellegentes ad quarum rerum significationem et praenuntiationem pertinerent. Hoc in eis culpat Apostolus, et in omnibus qui serviunt creaturae potius quam Creatori.

Nam nos quoque et dominicum diem et Pascha solemniter celebramus, et quaslibet alias christianas dierum festivitates. Sed quia intellegimus quo pertineant, non tempora observamus, sed quae illis significantur temporibus. Manichaei autem sic ea reprehendunt, quasi nullos dies et tempora observent. Sed cum de his interrogantur secundum opinionem sectae suae, omnia conantur exponere, ut non ipsa tempora, sed res, quarum illa signa sunt, observare videantur. Quas quidem res fabulosas esse atque falsissimas, aliis locis ostenditur. Nunc ad hoc dictum est, ut ore suo cogantur fateri, posse talia rationabiliter celebrari: et ideo circumcisionem carnis et recte impositam servis, et recte a liberis intellectam esse manifestum est. Repudiamus ergo eam carnalem cum Apostolo, et approbamus eam spiritalem cum Apostolo: et sabbati quietem non observamus in tempore; sed signum temporale intellegimus, et ad aeternam quietem quae illo signo significatur, aciem mentis intendimus. Repudiamus itaque temporum observationem cum Apostolo, et temporalium signorum intellegentiam tenemus cum Apostolo: duorumque Testamentorum differentiam sic probamus, ut in illo sint onera servorum, in isto gloria liberorum; in illo cognoscatur praefiguratio possessionis nostrae, in isto teneatur ipsa possessio. Interpretatur Apostolus sabbatum ad Hebraeos, cum dicit: Remanet igitur sabbatismus populo Dei. Interpretatur etiam circumcisionem, cum dicit de Abraham: Et signum accepit circumcisionis signaculum iustitiae fidei. Apostolicam itaque interpretationem spiritaliter teneo: carnalem servitutis observationem libertate contemno, utriusque Testamenti auctorem Deum venerans, qui et veteri homini fugienti tamquam dominus opposuit quod timeret, et novo redeunti tamquam pater aperuit quod amaret.

Nos illud, quod de inimicis occidendis illi populo dictum est, contrarium non esse dicimus praecepto evangelico de inimicis diligendis.

17. 1. De eo quod in Exodo scriptum est: Si aure audieris vocem meam, et facies quaecumque praecipio tibi; odero odientes te; et contristabo contristantes te: praecedet te angelus meus, et adducet te ad Amorrhaeum, et Pherezaeum, et Chananaeum, et Iebusaeum, et Gergesaeum; et occidetis illos. Deos eorum ne adoraveritis, neque feceritis opera ipsorum; sed eversione evertite illos, et delete eorum memoriam. His verbis de veteribus Libris ita commemoratis, tamquam contrarium opponit Adimantus quod in Evangelio scriptum est, dicente

Domino: Ego autem dico vobis: Diligite inimicos vestros, benedicite his qui vobis maledicunt, et benefacite iis qui vos oderunt, et orate pro iis qui vos persequuntur. Quo loco primo illud videndum est, quod satis esse debuerit homini volenti quasi contraria monstrare, quod de occidendis inimicis in veteri Lege scriptum esse commonuit. Dominus enim de inimicis diligendis, utique de hominibus praecepit; quos per nostram patientiam et caritatem ad salutem posse converti, et quivis intellegit, et exemplis saepissime demonstratum est. Quid ergo sibi vult, quod adiungenda consequentia putavit, ubi scriptum est: Deos eorum ne adoraveritis, neque feceritis opera ipsorum; sed eversione evertite illos, et delete eorum memoriam; nisi quia et deos Gentium Manichaei cogunt diligere? Et quod in Evangelio Dominus ait: Diligite inimicos vestros, non solum ad homines, sed ad daemonia quoque, vel etiam ad simulacra pertinere arbitrantur. Quod si ita est, quis non istam detestetur amentiam? Si autem non hoc arbitrantur, iste plurimum erravit, qui superstitiones Gentium evertendas esse praeceptas in Veteri Testamento commemorare voluit, cum in Novo quod scriptum est de inimicis diligendis, tamquam contrarium vellet opponere.

17. 2. Nos autem neque illud quod de hostibus hominibus occidendis in veteribus Libris illi populo dictum est contrarium esse dicimus huic praecepto evangelico, quo nobis ut inimicos nostros diligamus Dominus iubet: quandoquidem illa inimicorum interfectio carnali adhuc populo congruebat, cui Lex tamquam paedagogus data erat, sicut Apostolus dicit. Hi vero qui tunc in illo populo sancti et spiritales homines erant paucissimi, sicut Moyses, sicut Prophetae, quo animo facerent illam inimicorum interfectionem, et utrum eos quos interficiebant, diligerent, multum latet indoctos et impios, qui diligunt caecitatem suam; qui quoniam non sunt idonei videre ista, mole potius auctoritatis urgendi sunt. Quid enim est quod dicit Apostolus: Ego quidem absens corpore, praesens autem spiritu, iam iudicavi quasi praesens eum qui sic operatus est, in nomine Domini nostri Iesu Christi congregatis vobis et meo spiritu, cum potentia Domini Iesu, tradere eiusmodi satanae in interitum carnis, ut spiritus salvus sit in die Domini Iesu? Quid enim habet illa interfectio, quam multum isti exaggerant et invidiose ventilant, nisi interitum carnis? Sed quia exposuit Apostolus quo animo faceret, satis declaravit in aliquem inimicum vindictam cum caritate posse procedere. Et tamen hic etiam alio modo fortasse interitus carnis, qui fit per poenitentiam, potest intellegi. Ipsi

autem legunt scripturas apocryphas, quas etiam incorruptissimas esse dicunt, ubi scriptum est apostolum Thomam maledixisse homini, a quo per imprudentiam palma percussus est, ignorante quis esset, maledictumque illud continuo venisse ad effectum. Nam cum ille homo, quoniam minister convivii erat, ut apportaret aquam exisset ad fontem, a leone occisus et dilaniatus est. Quod ut manifestaretur ad aliorum terrorem, canis manum eius intulit mensis, ubi convivabatur Apostolus: atque ita cum causa quaereretur a nescientibus, eisque panderetur, in magnum timorem et magnum honorem Apostoli eos esse conversos; atque hinc Evangelii exordium commendandi exstitisse. Si vellet aliquis dentes Manichaeorum in ipsos convertere, quam mordaciter ista reprehenderet! Sed quia et ibi tacitum non est quo animo factum sit, videtur dilectio vindicantis. Sic etenim in illa scriptura legitur, quod deprecatus fuerit Apostolus pro illo in quem temporaliter vindicatum est, ut ei parceretur in futuro iudicio. Si ergo tempore Novi Testamenti, quo maxime caritas commendatur, de poenis visibilibus divinitus iniectus est carnalibus timor; quanto magis tempore Veteris Testamenti hoc congruisse illi populo intellegendum est, quem timor Legis tamquam paedagogi coercebat? Nam haec est brevissima et apertissima differentia duorum Testamentorum, timor et amor: illud ad veterem, hoc ad novum hominem pertinet; utrumque tamen unius Dei misericordissima dispensatione prolatum atque coniunctum. Et in veteri Scriptura tacetur animus vindicantium, quia paucissimi spiritales divinis revelationibus quid facerent, noverant, ut populus cui terror utilis erat, severissimo imperio domaretur: ut quemadmodum videbant dari in manus suas interficiendos inimicos impios cultoresque simulacrorum, sic ipsi formidarent in manus inimicorum suorum dari, si Dei veri iussa contemnerent, et ad cultum idolorum atque impietates Gentium laberentur. Nam et in ipsos similiter peccantes non dissimiliter vindicatum est. Sed omnis haec temporalis vindicta infirmos animos terret, ut enutritos sub disciplina erudiat, et a sempiternis atque ineffabilibus suppliciis possit avertere: quia plus timent carnales homines quod in praesenti Deus vindicat, quam illud quod futurum minatur.

17. 3. Potest ergo esse dilectio in vindicante. Quod unusquisque in filio suo probat, cum eum in mores pessimos defluentem, severissima coercitione constringit, et tanto magis, quanto magis eum diligit, atque hoc modo corrigi posse arbitratur. Non autem occidunt filios quos diligunt homines, quando eos corrigere volunt: quia multi hanc vitam pro magno bono habent, et totum

quare volunt educare filios suos, in hac vita sperant. Fideles autem atque sapientes homines, qui credunt esse aliam vitam meliorem, et quanta possunt ex parte noverunt; nec ipsi vindicant occidendo, cum filios suos volunt corrigere, quia in hac vita eos posse corrigi credunt: Deus autem qui novit quid cuique tribuat, vindicat occidendo in quos voluerit, sive per homines, sive occulto rerum ordine; non quia eos odit in quantum homines sunt, sed in quantum peccatores sunt. Nam in ipsis veteribus Libris legimus dictum Deo: Et nihil odisti eorum quae fecisti; sed omnia, sive per poenas sive per praemia iustitia moderante disponit. Nonne apostolus Paulus Christianis fidelibus loquebatur, cum diceret: Probet autem se homo, et sic de pane edat, et de calice bibat. Qui enim manducat et bibit indigne, iudicium sibi manducat et bibit, non diiudicans corpus Domini. Propterea in vobis multi infirmi et aegri, et dormiunt sufficientes. Si autem nos ipsos diiudicaremus, non utique diiudicaremur. Dum iudicamur autem, a Domino corripimur, ne cum mundo damnemur? Ecce manifestum est Deum cum dilectione corrigere, non solum infirmitatibus et aegritudinibus, sed etiam mortibus temporalibus, eos quos non vult damnare cum mundo.

17. 4. Attendant haec isti, et videant quomodo potuerint et impiae gentes dari in manus populi, quamvis adhuc carnalis, tamen unum Deum colentis, ut ab eo interficerentur; cum in eo tamen populo si qui essent spiritales, sine alicuius odio intellegerent dispensationem Dei: et quomodo non sit contrarium quod Dominus nobis in Evangelio praecepit, ut diligamus inimicos nostros: de quibus tamen promittit ipse vindictam, cum de illo iudice similitudinem inducit, qui quotidianas interpellationes viduae mulieris petentis ut se vindicaret, quamvis esset iniustus, nec Deum timens, nec homines reverens, tamen sustinere non potuit, et audivit eam, ne ulterius taedium pateretur: ex cuius comparatione multo magis Deum, qui est benignissimus atque iustissimus, dixit vindicare electos suos de inimicis eorum. Huic isti audeant obicere quaestionem, et dicant, si possunt: Quid est, quod iussisti ut inimicos nostros diligamus, et de illis nos vindicare disponis? An forte contra voluntatem suorum sanctorum facturus est, eos quos illi diligunt, puniendo atque damnando? Imo ipsi potius ab ista calumniosa caecitate convertantur ad Deum, et in utroque Testamento intellegant eius voluntatem, ne in sinistra parte inveniantur inter eos quibus dicturus est Dominus: Ite in ignem aeternum, qui praeparatus est diabolo et angelis eius. Esurivi enim et non

dedistis mihi manducare; et cetera talia. Displicet enim istis miseris, quod Deus populo suo interficiendos tradidit inimicos; et ipsi panem mendicanti dari prohibent, non inimico, sed supplici. Intellegant potius sine odio esse posse vindictam, quam pauci intellegunt: et tamen quamdiu non intellegitur, tamdiu necesse est, ut lector in libris utriusque Testamenti magno labore aut errore iactetur, et putet contrarias sibi esse Scripturas.

17. 5. Quam vindictam sine odio nondum Apostoli animo ceperant, quando irati eis a quibus non recipiebantur hospitio, quaesiverunt de Domino utrum vellet eos petere ignem de coelo, sicut Elias fecerat, quo igne homines inhospitales consumerentur. Tunc respondit eis Dominus, dicens eos nescire cuius spiritus filii essent, et quod ipse liberare venisset, non perdere: quoniam illi animo inimico perdere cupiebant eos, quos volebant igne consumi. Postea vero cum impleti essent Spiritu sancto, et perfecti facti essent, qui iam possent etiam inimicos diligere, acceperunt potestatem vindicandi, quia iam sine odio poterant vindicare. Qua potestate Petrus apostolus usus est in eo libro quem isti non accipiunt, quoniam manifeste continet Paracleti adventum, id est, consolatoris sancti Spiritus, quem lugentibus misit, cum ab eorum oculis ipse ascendisset in coelum. Consolator enim tristibus mittitur, secundum illam eiusdem Domini sententiam: Beati lugentes, quoniam ipsi consolabuntur. Ipse etiam dicit: Tunc lugebunt filii sponsi, cum ablatus fuerit ab eis sponsus. In illo ergo libro, ubi apertissime Spiritus sanctus, quem Dominus consolatorem promiserat, venisse declaratur, legimus ad sententiam Petri cecidisse homines, et mortuos esse virum et uxorem, qui mentiri ausi erant Spiritui sancto. Quod isti magna caecitate vituperant, cum in apocryphis pro magno legant, et illud quod de apostolo Thoma commemoravi, et ipsius Petri filiam paralyticam factam precibus patris, et hortulani filiam ad precem ipsius Petri esse mortuam; et respondent, quod hoc eis expediebat, ut et illa solveretur paralysi, et illa moreretur: tamen ad preces Apostoli factum esse non negant. Quis autem illis dixit: Non expediebat gentibus impiis interfici, quas traditas esse divinitus in manus populi Iudaeorum irridentes mirari se fingunt? Cum autem illa non odio, sed bono animo Apostoli fecerint; unde isti convincunt animos virorum spiritalium qui in illo populo fuerunt, quod eos oderant, qui per ipsos divina iustitia de hac vita iubebantur auferri? Compescant potius temeritatem suam, et non decipiant imperitos, quibus aut non vacat legere, aut nolunt legere, aut perverso animo legunt; et non attendunt et misericordiam et severitatem Dei,

utriusque Testamenti litteris commendari. Nam de inimici dilectione, ut non reddatur malum pro malo, in veteribus Libris legitur: Domine Deus meus, si feci istud, si est iniquitas in manibus meis. Si reddidi retribuentibus mihi mala, decidam merito ab inimicis meis inanis. Quis hoc diceret, nisi qui sciret hoc Deo placere, ut malum pro malo nemo reddat? Sed hoc perfectorum est, ut non oderint in peccatoribus nisi peccata, ipsos autem homines diligant; et cum vindicant, non vindicent acerbitate saevitiae, sed moderatione iustitiae; ne ipsa relaxatio peccati plus noceat peccatori, quam poena vindictae. Nec tamen hoc fecerunt iusti homines, nisi auctoritate divina; ne quis arbitretur passim sibi esse permissum necare quem velit, aut iudicio persequi, aut poenis quibuslibet affligere. Aliquando autem aperte ponitur in Scripturis ipsa divina auctoritas, aliquando autem occultatur, ut et manifestis lector instruatur, et exerceatur obscuris.

17. 6. Certe inimicum et persecutorem suum nimis ingratum et nimis infestum Saul regem accepit David in potestatem, ut ei faceret quod vellet; et elegit parcere potius, quam occidere. Non enim erat iussus occidere, sed neque prohibitus: imo etiam divinitus audierat se impune facere quidquid vellet inimico; et tamen tantam potestatem ad mansuetudinem contulit. Dicatur mihi quem timuit, cum interficere noluit. Nec hominem possumus dicere timuisse, quem acceperat in potestatem; nec Deum, qui dederat. Ubi ergo nec difficultas fuit occidendi, nec timor, dilectio pepercit inimico. Ecce David ille bellator implevit praeceptum Christi, quod accepimus, ut diligamus inimicos. Atque utinam hoc imitarentur isti, qui humanum affectum misericordiae ad nescio quae crudelia deliramenta torserunt! Dum enim credunt panem plorare, quod fieri non potest, non eum porrigunt homini, quem plorantem vident. Fortassis dicant, sicut solent caeci iactare insana convicia, meliorem fuisse David qui pepercit inimico, quam Deum qui dederit ei occidendi potestatem: quasi vero Deus nescierit cui dederit hanc potestatem. Noverat utique voluntatem servi sui, sed ut ceteris etiam hominibus ad imitandum innotesceret ea quae in corde David iam Deo nota erat inimici dilectio, dedit illi in potestatem inimicum, quem nondum volebat occidi, propter certam rerum dispensationem, quam per illum impleri oportebat. Ita et David bonitas commendata est, ut haberent homines quod amarent; et Saulis regis malitia ad exitum digniorem dilata est, ut haberent homines quod timerent.

Quod bona temporalia contempta esse in libris Novi et Veteris Testamenti demonstratur.

18. 1. De eo quod in Deuteronomio scriptum est: Si aure audieris vocem Domini Dei tui, benedictus es in agro tuo, benedictus es in prato tuo, benedictus fructus ventris tui, et fructus terrae tuae, et generationes iumentorum tuorum, et armentum boum tuorum, et grex ovium tuarum; benedictus es in introitu tuo et egressu. Huic capitulo illud dicunt in Evangelio esse contrarium: Si quis vult me sequi, abneget semetipsum sibi, et tollat crucem suam, et sequatur me. Quid enim prodest homini, si totum mundum lucretur, animae autem suae detrimentum patiatur? Aut quam dabit homo commutationem pro anima sua? Sed ex illa regula ostenditur non esse contrarium, qua notum esse iam debet, carnali adhuc populo congruenter carnalia et temporalia praemia fuisse promissa, sed tamen ab uno Deo, cuius est creatura omnis et superior et inferior. Certe enim ipse Adimantus posuit testimonium de Evangelio, ubi Dominus ait: Nolite iurare, neque per coelum, quia thronus eius est; neque per terram, quia scabellum est pedum eius. Quod quidem et in veteribus Libris scriptum est: Coelum mihi thronus est, terra scabellum pedum meorum. Quid ergo mirum si bona throni sui dat spiritaliter sibi servientibus, et bona scabelli pedum suorum dat carnaliter sibi servientibus; cum spiritus superior sit, et caro inferior, sicut superiora sunt coelestia, et inferiora terrestria? Quamquam illa omnia, id est, ager, et pratum, et fructus ventris, et fructus terrae, et iumentorum, et armentum boum, et grex ovium possint etiam spiritaliter intellegi. Sed nunc ad rem non pertinet ista tractatio. Si autem in ipso Novo Testamento, cuius praemium et haereditas ad novum hominem pertinet, tamen et Dominus iisdem ipsis quos vult esse rerum temporalium contemptores, ut in Evangelio sibi serviant, promittit multiplicationem earumdem rerum in hoc saeculo, dicens quod accipient in hoc saeculo centies tantum, in saeculo autem venturo vitam aeternam; sicut etiam in veteri Scriptura dicitur: Fideli homini totus mundus divitiarum est. Unde exsultat Apostolus dicens: Quasi nihil habentes, et omnia possidentes; si ergo in Novo Testamento praeter aeternam possessionem quae promittitur sanctis, huius quoque possessionis quae transitura est, multiplicatio non subtrahitur, et tanto fit uberior, quanto contemptius possidetur; quanto magis in Veteri Testamento carnalis populi praemia talia esse debuerunt, ipso tamen

uno et vero Deo gubernatore omnium temporum omnia pro tempore moderante et administrante.

18. 2. Sed ne in solis Novi Testamenti libris isti arbitrentur haec esse contempta, audiant prophetam abicientem talem felicitatem, et ad unum Dominum Deum confugiendum esse cantantem. Ita enim dicit: De gladio maligno erue me, et exime me de manu filiorum alienorum, quorum os locutum est vanitatem, et dextera eorum dextera iniquitatis. Quorum filii ipsorum velut novellae constabilitae in iuventute sua. Filiae eorum compositae et ornatae velut similitudo templi. Cellaria eorum plena, eructantia ex hoc in hoc. Oves eorum fecundae, multiplicantes in exitibus suis; boves eorum crassae. Non est ruina sepis, nec exitus, neque clamor in plateis eorum. Beatum dixerunt populum cui haec sunt; beatus populus cuius Dominus Deus ipsius. Attendant ergo quomodo irrideatur ista felicitas in hominibus impiis, et tota beatitudo in Deo solo inconcussa figatur. Illi enim dicunt beatum populum cui haec sunt; sed beatus populus cuius est Dominus Deus ipsius. Quod autem etiam illud contrarium esse putaverunt huic loco Veteris Testamenti, quod Dominus ait: Omnis qui confusus fuerit me aut verba mea in gente ista adultera et peccatrice, et Filius hominis confundetur illum, cum venerit in gloria Patris sui et laude sanctorum angelorum suorum; quod pertineat ad contemptum rerum temporalium non video. Quod si propterea pertinet, ne aliquis territus de talium rerum damnis, Christum confiteri aut erubescat, aut timeat, quid habent quod dicant? Cum et nos dicimus ita esse ista munera Dei, ut tamen sint infima, et in comparatione salutaris confessionis, non solum amittenda, sed ultro etiam proicienda: carnalibus tamen haec amantibus, et nondum capientibus promissa coelestia, ne ab idolis et daemonibus ista peterent, utiliter a Domino Deo esse pollicita.

Omnia in utriusque Testamenti scripturis, et ad expetendum et ad fugiendum, et ad sumendum et ad reiciendum sibi concordantia et suis gradibus ordinata.

19. 1. De eo quod scriptum est in Lege: Ego sum qui divitias do amicis meis, et paupertatem inimicis meis. Huic sententiae illud opponunt quod Dominus dicit: Beati pauperes spiritu, quoniam ipsorum est regnum coelorum; et: Vae vobis divitibus, quia percepistis consolationem vestram. Sed cur nolunt et alia

in Evangelio contueri? Ubi enim scriptum est: Beati pauperes spiritu, quoniam ipsorum est regnum coelorum; ibi sequitur: Beati mites, quoniam ipsi haereditate possidebunt terram. Ecce habent amicos Dei haereditate terrae divites fieri. Cum autem ad tantam egestatem dives ille redigitur, ut ab eo paupere quem neglexerat, digito brevi in aqua tincto arenti linguae suae humorem stillari deprecetur, intellegant quomodo fiant pauperes inimici Dei, et id esse cognoscant quod in Lege scriptum est: Ego sum qui divitias do amicis meis, et paupertatem inimicis meis.

19. 2. Nam istas divitias temporales et in veteri Scriptura esse contemptas et superius docui, et innumerabilibus locis qui legere voluerit, inveniet. Unde est etiam illud: Melius est modicum iusto, super divitias peccatorum multas. Et illud: Bonum mihi lex oris tui, super millia auri et argenti. Et illud: Iudicia Dei vera iustificata in idipsum, desiderabilia super aurum et lapidem pretiosum multum. Et illud: Beatus vir qui invenit sapientiam, et immortalis qui videt prudentiam. Melius est enim illam mercari, quam auri et argenti thesauros. Pretiosior est autem lapidibus optimis, non resistit illi ullum malum; bene nota est omnibus appropinquantibus ei, et eis qui considerant eam diligenter. Omne autem pretiosum non est illi dignum. Et illud: Propter hoc optavi, et datus est mihi sensus, et invocavi, et venit in me spiritus sapientiae. Et praeposui illam regnis et sedibus, et honestatem nihil esse duxi ad comparationem ipsius. Nec comparavi illi lapidem pretiosum: quoniam omne aurum in comparatione illius arena est exigua, et tamquam lutum aestimabitur argentum ad illam. Haec isti si aut legerent aut non impie legerent, viderent omnia in utriusque Testamenti scripturis, et ad expetendum et ad fugiendum, et ad sumendum et ad reiciendum sibi concordantia et suis gradibus ordinata.

In natura humana, quae peccato in inferiora defluxit, ea quae Deus carnalibus figurata promittit, spiritalibus aperta monstrat.

20. 1. De eo quod scriptum est in Lege: Si ambulaveritis in lege, et praecepta mea custodieritis; dabo pluvias tempore suo, et producet terra fructus suos, et arbores poma, et vindemiae tuae messibus succedent, et satio vindemiis: et saturabimini, et sedebitis in pace in terra vestra, et dormietis, et non erit qui vos terreat: et perdam omnem belluam ex terra vestra; et persequemini inimicos

vestros, et cadent ante vos in gladio: et insequentur quinque ex vobis centum, et centum ex vobis persequentur decem millia, et concident inimici vestri ante vos in gladio: et veniam, et benedicam vos, et multiplicabo vos, et disponam vos. Manducabitis vetus quod inveteravit, et proicietis vetus ante novum. Iam neminem oportet postulare a nobis, ut haec ostendamus quam congruenter illi populo Deus promiserit. Multa enim de hac re diximus, et cui parva sunt, nimis tardus est. Sed tamen quod etiam huic loco de Novo Testamento dicunt esse contrarium; illud videlicet quod Dominus ait: Nolite portare aurum, neque argentum, neque nummos in zonis vestris; non peram in via, neque duas tunicas, neque calceamenta, neque virgam; dignus est enim operarius mercede sua: quid mirum si haec Evangelistis donaverit? Numquid in hoc ministerium populus Iudaicus vocabatur? Quae tamen omnia spiritaliter perscrutanda sunt, ne ipse Dominus hominibus impiis contra sua praecepta fecisse videatur, qui etiam loculos habebat, quibus ad necessarium victum pecunia portabatur. Nisi forte dicturi sunt in zonis habere pecuniam, peccatum esse; in loculis autem, non esse peccatum. Non autem ista iussa, sed permissa esse Apostolis, ex hoc intellegitur, quod apostolus Paulus manibus suis operatus victum quaerebat, non abusus ea potestate, sicut ipse loquitur, quam Dominus Evangelistis dedit. Quod enim permittitur a Domino, etiam non facere licet: quod autem iubetur, nisi fiat peccatum est.

20. 2. Addunt etiam de illo divite, cui Deus dixerat: Stulte, hac nocte a te animam tuam expetam; quae autem praeparasti, cuius erunt? et dicunt non minus huic capitulo Legis esse contrarium: cum in isto inanitas irrisa sit vanae laetitiae, quia incerta illa pro certis habuit; populo autem Israel certam faciebat illam pollicitationem omnipotentia pollicentis. Unde apostolus Paulus scribens ad Timotheum, de divitibus saeculi huius, quos noverat in Ecclesiae membris habere suum locum, ita loquitur: Divitibus huius saeculi praecipe, non superbe sapere, neque sperare in incerto divitiarum, sed in Deo vivo, qui praestat nobis omnia abundanter ad fruendum: benefaciant, divites sint in operibus bonis, facile tribuant, communicent, thesaurizent sibi fundamentum bonum in futurum, ut apprehendant veram vitam. Quis hic non intellegat non esse culpabile habere ista, sed amare et spem in eis ponere, et ea praeferre aut etiam conferre veritati, iustitiae, sapientiae, fidei, bonae conscientiae, caritati Dei et proximi, quibus omnibus anima pia dives est in secretis suis coram oculis Dei? Sed ut diligatur Deus, qui diligentibus se ista cuncta et invisibilia et aeterna

largitur, id est, se ipsum his omnibus plenum donat dilectoribus suis: ut ergo ipse diligatur, illo etiam tempore quo carnalis anima, carnis videlicet affectibus implicata, nisi temporalia desiderare non novit, persuadendum illi est, quod etiam ista Deus dat homini; quia et verum est, et utilissime creditur. Hoc populo Israel factum est per illas pollicitationes, quas imperitissime miseri derident, ut etiam in ipsis infimis rebus, quomodo possent, Deum diligere assuescerent, quamvis plus ibi operetur timor. Quae tamen omnia dona temporalia figurae sunt donorum aeternorum, et illa de inimicis victoria praesignat victoriam de diabolo et angelis eius.

20. 3. Et quod isti adiecerunt quasi contrarium Veteri Testamento, quod Apostolus loquitur, Deum non pugna et dissensione, sed pace delectari: sciant talem Deum praedicari in Scripturis illis, cui pacem suam nemo possit auferre; non qualem ipsi praedicant, qui timens ne irrueret bellum regionibus suis, membra sua longe misit, ut peregrina bella tolerarent, et postea liberari atque purgari victa et inquinata non possent. In natura vero humana, quae peccato in inferiora defluxit, ita Deus pace delectatur, ut non relinquat libramenta iustitiae, nec pacem quam diligit velit calcari a peccantibus, sed amari a certantibus, apprehendi a victoribus, et ea carnalibus figurata promittere, spiritalibus aperta monstrare.

Absurdum non est, quod in veterem hominem maledictum prolatum est, quem Dominus suspendit in ligno.

21. De eo quod scriptum est in Deuteronomio: Maledictus omnis qui in ligno pependerit. Licet saepe a Manichaeis ista quaestio ventilata sit, non video tamen quid habeat huic sententiae contrarium quod ex Evangelio Adimantus opponendum putavit, ubi Dominus ait: Si vis perfectus esse, vende omnia quaecumque possides, et divide pauperibus, et tolle crucem tuam, et sequere me. Hicpraeterquam quod crucem nominat, nihil attendit esse contrarium ei quod dictum est: Maledictus omnis qui in ligno pependerit: quasi vero talem crucem possit quisque tollere et sequi Dominum. Sed illa tollitur, cum sequimur Dominum, de qua dicit Apostolus: Qui autem Iesu Christi sunt, carnem suam crucifixerunt cum passionibus et concupiscentiis. Tali enim cruce vetus homo, id est, vetus vita perimitur, quam de Adam traximus, ut quod in

illo fuit voluntarium, in nobis fieret naturale. Quod ostendit Apostolus dicens: Fuimus et nos aliquando natura filii irae, sicut et ceteri. Si ergo vetus vita de Adam, unde et nomine veteris hominis vetus vita significatur; quid absurdum habet, quod in veterem hominem maledictum prolatum est, quem Dominus suspendit in ligno? Quia ex ipsa successione mortalitatem gestavit, de virgine Maria mortaliter natus, habens carnem non peccatricem, sed tamen similitudinem gerentem carnis peccati; quia mori poterat, et mors de peccato est. Unde etiam est illud: Scientes quia vetus homo noster simul confixus est cruci cum illo, ut evacuetur corpus peccati. Non ergo Dominus per linguam Moysi famuli Dei, sed mors ipsa meruit maledictum, quam Dominus noster suscipiendo evacuavit. Mors itaque illa pependit in ligno, quae per mulierem ad hominem serpentina persuasione pervenit. Unde etiam serpentem, ad significationem ipsius mortis, Moyses in eremo exaltavit in ligno. Et quoniam a mortiferis cupiditatibus per fidem sanamur crucis Domini, qua cruce mors ligno suspensa est; propterea qui serpentum morsibus venenabantur, conspecto serpente qui fixus erat atque exaltatus in ligno, continuo sanabantur. Huic sacramento ipse Dominus attestatus est dicens: Sicut enim Moyses exaltavit serpentem in eremo, ita exaltari oportet Filium hominis. Suscipiendo autem ignominiosissimum apud homines mortis genus Dominus noster Iesus Christus, hoc est, mortem crucis, commendavit nobis dilectionem suam, ut merito Apostolus diceret, accendens nos in eius caritatem: Christus nos redemit de maledicto Legis, factus pro nobis maledictum. Scriptum est enim: Maledictus omnis qui pendet in ligno. Ut non solum nullam mortem, sed etiam nullum mortis genus Christiana libertas, sicut Iudaica servitus, formidaret.

Sicut tempore caritatis bonitas, sic tempore timoris severitas Dei.

22. De homine quem lapidari Deus iussit, qui sabbato inventus est ligna colligere. Dominus in Evangelio ubi hominis manum aridam sanavit die sabbati, divinum opus fecit, non humanum; nec ab otio recessit qui iussit et factum est. Et ideo non est simile hoc factum ligna colligenti, quod facere cum inventus esset homo die sabbati, iussu Dei lapidatus est. De servili autem observatione sabbati, et de vindicta temporalis mortis, iam multa dicta sunt. Sicut enim tempore caritatis bonitas, sic tempore timoris severitas Dei maxime commendatur. Et cum adhuc non oporteret ante adventum Domini nudare

populo legitimarum sacramenta figurarum, non invitabantur illi homines significata intellegere, sed iussa cogebantur implere: nondum enim Deo inhaerebant per spiritum, sed per carnem legi serviebant. Miror autem quod isti plangunt lapidatum hominem Dei praecepto, quia contra iussum Legis ligna collegit, et non plangunt arborem arefactam verbo Christi, quae contra nullum praeceptum fecerat; cum talem animam arboris esse credant, qualem hominis.

Fecunditas et continentia.

23. De eo quod scriptum est: Mulier tua sicut vinea frondescens, et filii tui ut novellae olivarum in circuitu mensae tuae, et videbis filios filiorum tuorum; et scies quia hoc modo benedicitur homo qui timet Dominum. Hoc per prophetam figurate dictum, et ad significationem Ecclesiae pertinere Manichaei non intellegunt, et putant contrarium esse quod in Evangelio Dominus de spadonibus ait, qui se ipsos castrant propter regnum coelorum. Sed nos iam et de viro, et de uxore, et de spadonibus, quantum satis fuit, in tertio capitulo disseruimus.

Non in pane solo vivit homo, sed in omni verbo Dei.

24. De eo quod scriptum est apud Salomonem: Imitare formicam, et intuere diligentiam eius, quia ab aestatis tempore usque ad hiemem colligit sibi alimonias. Neque hoc intellegunt Manichaei spiritaliter esse accipiendum, et putant praeceptum esse ut thesaurizemus in terra, aut etiam curemus haec horrea, quae sine ullo praecepto multum homines implere festinant. Et ideo illud Adimantus ex Evangelio dicit adversum esse huic sententiae, ubi Dominus ait: Nolite cogitare de crastino. Sed neque hoc intellegunt ad id pertinere, ut temporalia non amemus, neque timeamus ne nobis desint necessaria, et propter ipsa conquirenda vel Deo vel hominibus serviamus. Nam si hoc ideo dictum est, ut non servetur panis in crastinum, magis hoc implent vagi Romanorum, quos Passivos appellant, qui annona quotidiana satiato ventre, aut donant statim quod restat, aut proiciunt, quam vel Domini discipuli, qui etiam cum ipso Domino coeli et terrae in terra ambulantes loculos habebant; vel Paulus apostolus, qui omnium terrenorum contemptor, sic tamen gubernavit ea quae

praesenti vitae erant necessaria, ut etiam de viduis praeceperit dicens: Si quis fidelis habet viduas, sufficienter tribuat illis, ut non gravetur Ecclesia, quo veris viduis sufficere possit. Sed tamen illud de formica ita positum est, ut quemadmodum illa aestate colligit unde in hieme pascatur, sic unusquisque Christianus in rerum tranquillitate, quam significat aestas, colligat verbum Dei, ut in adversitate et tribulationibus, quae hiemis nomine significantur, habeat unde spiritaliter vivat. Non enim in pane solo vivit homo, sed in omni verbo Dei. Si autem hoc eos movet, quod in terra condit formica quod colligit; irascantur etiam illi thesauro quem Dominus in agro dicit inventum.

Propheticae sententiae non repugnat quod Adimantus posuit ex Evangelio.

25. De eo quod scriptum est in Osee: Da illis ventrem vacuum et ubera arida: mortifica semen ventris ipsorum, ne pariant. Et haec prophetica locutio est utique figurata. Nam et ventrem non carneum intellegunt in Evangelio, cum legunt: Flumina aquae vivae fluent de ventre eius. Et ubera quaedam habebat Apostolus, cum diceret: Lac vobis potum dedi, non escam; et iterum: Factus sum parvulus in medio vestrum, tamquam si nutrix fovens filios suos. Et Galatas ad carnalia declinantes iterum parturit, donec Christus in eis formetur. Et ideo huic propheticae sententiae non repugnat quod Adimantus posuit ex Evangelio, quod in resurrectione a mortuis, neque nubent, neque uxores ducent, neque morientur, sed sunt ut Angeli Dei. Nam hoc est utique quod accipiunt etiam spadones, de quibus Isaias loquitur: Locum nominatum multo meliorem filiorum et filiarum, nomen aeternum dabo eis, inquit. Non ergo isti arbitrentur in solo Evangelio tale praemium promitti sanctis: ventremque vacuum et ubera arida et mortificatum semen, ne pariant, intellegant de his esse dictum de quibus dicit Apostolus: Sicut enim Iamnes et Iambres restiterunt Moysi, sic et isti resistunt veritati, homines mente corrupti, reprobi circa fidem: sed ultra non proficient; dementia enim eorum manifesta erit omnibus, sicut et illorum fuit. Cum ergo ultra non proficient, tunc habebunt ventrem vacuum, et ubera arida, et mortificatum semen. In qua sententia se isti tamquam in speculo dignentur inspicere.

Dupliciter appellatur malum: unum quod homo facit, alterum quod patitur.

26. De eo quod scriptum est in Amos propheta: Si fieri potest ut ambulantes duo in via minime se agnoscant, et leo sine praeda ad catulum suum revertatur; si decidet avis sine aucupe in terram, si tendunt muscipulam sine causa, ut nihil capiant; si dabit sonum tuba in civitate, ut plebs non terreatur: ita etiam malum aliquod in civitate non perpetratur, quod Dominus non faciet. Malum hoc loco non peccatum, sed poena intellegenda est. Dupliciter enim appellatur malum; unum quod homo facit, alterum quod patitur: quod facit, peccatum est; quod patitur, poena. De poenis ergo loquebatur Propheta, cum hoc diceret. Divina enim providentia cuncta moderante et gubernante, ita homo male facit quod vult, ut male patiatur quod non vult. Sic autem isti accusant Prophetam ista dicentem, quasi in Evangelio non legerint: Nonne duo passeres asse veneunt, et unus ex his non cadit in terram sine Patris vestri voluntate? Ita ergo Deus malum facit, quod non ipsi Deo malum est, sed eis in quos vindicat. Itaque ipse, quantum ad se pertinet, bonum facit; quia omne iustum bonum est, et iusta est illa vindicta. Et ideo non est contrarium, quod Adimantus obicit dixisse Dominum: Arbor bona fructus bonos facit; mala autem arbor malos fructus facit. Quamvis enim malum sit gehenna damnato; iustitia tamen Dei bona est, et ipse fructus est ex arbore bona. Ille autem malis peccatorum suorum thesaurizat sibi iram in die irae et revelationis iusti iudicii Dei, qui reddet unicuique secundum opera sua. Quamquam istae duae arbores manifestissime in similitudine duorum hominum positae sint, id est, iusti et iniusti: quia nisi quisque voluntatem mutaverit, bonum operari non potest. Quod in nostra potestate esse positum, alio loco docet, ubi ait: Aut facite arborem bonam, et fructum eius bonum; aut facite arborem malam, et fructum eius malum. Illis enim hoc dicit, qui putabant se bona loqui posse, cum essent mali, hoc est, bonos fructus facere, cum essent arbores malae. Sic enim et subiungit: Hypocritae, quomodo potestis bona loqui, cum mali sitis? Mala ergo arbor fructus bonos facere non potest: sed ex mala fieri bona potest, ut bonos fructus ferat. Fuistis enim aliquando tenebrae, inquit Apostolus; nunc autem lux in Domino. Tamquam si diceret: Fuistis aliquando arbores malae, et ideo non poteratis tunc nisi malos fructus facere: nunc autem lux in Domino, id est, et iam facti arbores bonae, date fructus bonos; quod sequitur dicens: Sicut filii lucis ambulate: fructus enim luminis est in omni iustitia et veritate; probantes quid sit beneplacitum Domino. Nam et in ipso Evangelii capitulo, si non studio malevolentiae fugeret Adimantus, posset advertere quomodo dicatur Deus malum facere. Ibi enim ait Dominus, quod etiam iste commemoravit: Omnis arbor quae non facit fructus bonos, excidetur, et in ignem mittetur.

Haec sunt mala quae Deus facit, id est, peccatoribus poenas, quod in ignem mittet arbores, quae in malitia perseverantes fieri bonae noluerint, cum hoc ipsis arboribus malum sit. Deus autem, ut saepe dixi, non dat fructus malos, quia iustitiae fructus est vindicta peccati.

In nostra potestate est, ut vel inseri Dei bonitate, vel excidi severitate mereamur.

27. De eo quod in Isaia propheta scriptum est: Ego sum Deus qui facio pacem, et constituo mala. Etiam hoc eadem regula solvitur. Non enim reprehendit Adimantus quod dixit Deus, facio pacem; sed quod dixit, constituo mala. Cum Paulus apostolus haec duo similiter uno in loco etiam latius tractaverit dicens: Vides ergo bonitatem et severitatem Dei: in eos quidem qui ceciderunt, severitatem; in te autem bonitatem, si permanseris in bonitate: alioquin et tu excideris, et illi si non permanserint in incredulitate, inserentur. Potens est enim Deus iterum inserere illos. In hoc sermone apostolico satis apparet bonitas Dei, secundum quam dixit Isaias: Ego sum Deus qui facio pacem; et severitas, secundum quam dixit, constituo mala. Simul etiam ostendit in nostra potestate esse, ut vel inseri bonitate ipsius, vel excidi severitate mereamur. Non ergo est Isaiae contrarium Evangelium, sicut putat, vel potius putari cupit Adimantus, ubi Dominus ait: Beati pacifici, quia filii Dei vocabuntur. Vel ex ipsa enim parte debuit agnoscere, etiam Isaiam scire filios Dei esse pacificos, quia per eum dixit Deus: Ego sum qui facio pacem. Sed cum in alia parte ad male intellegendum oculum fixit, in altera se ipse excaecavit. Quod si vellet alius similiter caecus dicere bonum esse Vetus Testamentum, ubi dicit Deus: Nolo mortem peccatoris, quantum ut revertatur et vivat; malum autem esse Novum Testamentum, ubi dicit Christus: Ite in ignem aeternum, qui praeparatus est diabolo et angelis eius: nonne in foveam cadens omnes qui se sequerentur, indoctos et Scripturarum ignaros in imperitiae caecitatem germinante malitia secum pariter praecipitaret? Qui autem oculo pio legit, et in Novo Testamento invenit quod isti accusant in Vetere, et in Vetere quod laudant in Novo.

Ea quae oculis corporeis sunt invisibilia, menti vero visibilia fatemur.

28. 1. De eo quod scriptum est in Isaia: Et factum est eo anno quo mortuus est Ozias rex, vidi Dominum sedentem in sede altissima; et plena erat domus gloriae ipsius, et in circuitu Seraphim stabant, senas alas habentes, et binis quidem operiebant faciem ipsius, binis vero pedes. Huic loco illud opponit Adimantus, quod ait Apostolus: Regi autem saeculorum invisibili honor et laus in saecula. In qua quaestione quaerendum est, quid ei visum fuerit; vel in illa visione Isaiae binas alas praetermittere, quibus volabant Seraphim, dicentes: Sanctus, sanctus, sanctus Dominus Deus sabaoth: vel in Apostoli verbis non totum dicere. Nam ita dicit Apostolus: Regi autem saeculorum invisibili, incorruptibili, soli Deo honor et gloria in saecula saeculorum. An forte timuit ne Trinitatis commemoratio commendaret Prophetam lectori, et aliquid magnum ibi latere suspicaretur? Ter enim dicitur: Sanctus, sanctus, sanctus Dominus Deus sabaoth. In Apostolo autem forte vidit, quod si dixisset, incorruptibili Deo; responderetur illi quod nunc istis dicimus: Quid ergo incorruptibili Deo factura erat gens tenebrarum, si cum ea pugnare noluisset? Aut si forte mendosos codices legerat, aut iste mendosus est ubi nos ipsum Adimantum legimus, non est diutius de re dubia disserendum: sed iam quaerendum est quomodo et Propheta dixerit vidisse se Deum in sede altissima, et apostolus Paulus verum dixerit, invisibilem Deum. Interrogo itaque istos utrum invisibilia possint conspici. Si dicunt posse; quid ergo calumniantur, si Deum invisibilem Propheta conspexit? Si autem dicunt non posse, ipsi Apostolo potius calumnientur, si audent, qui ait: Invisibilia enim Dei, a constitutione mundi, per ea quae facta sunt, intellecta conspiciuntur. Ipse enim dixit esse invisibilia; et ipse rursus dicit, conspiciuntur. Nonne hic coguntur fateri oculis corporeis esse invisibilia, menti vero esse visibilia? Sic igitur et Propheta

Deum, qui corporaliter invisibilis est, non corporaliter, sed spiritaliter vidit.

28. 2. Nam multa genera visionis in Scripturis sanctis inveniuntur. Unum, secundum oculos corporis; sicut vidit Abraham tres viros sub ilice Mambre, et Moyses ignem in rubo, et discipuli transfiguratum Dominum in monte inter Moysen et Eliam: et cetera huiusmodi. Alterum, secundum spiritum, quo imaginamur ea quae per corpus sentimus: nam et pars ipsa nostra cum divinitus assumitur, multa revelantur, non per oculos corporis, aut aures, aliumve sensum carnalem; sed tamen his similia, sicut vidit Petrus discum illum

submitti e coelo cum variis animalibus. Ex hoc genere est etiam istud Isaiae, quod imperitissime impii reprehendunt. Non enim Deum forma corporea circumterminat: sed quemadmodum figurate, non proprie, multa dicuntur; ita etiam figurate multa monstrantur. Tertium autem genus visionis est secundum mentis intuitum, quo intellecta conspiciuntur veritas atque sapientia: sine quo genere illa duo quae prius posui, vel infructuosa sunt, vel etiam in errorem mittunt. Cum enim ea, quae sive corporeis sensibus, sive illi parti animae quae corporalium rerum imagines capit, divinitus demonstrantur, non solum sentiuntur his modis, sed etiam mente intelleguntur, tunc est perfecta revelatio. Ex hoc tertio genere est visio illa quam commemoravi, dicente Apostolo: Invisibilia enim Dei, a constitutione mundi, per ea quae facta sunt, intellecta conspiciuntur. Hac visione videtur Deus, cum per pietatem fidei et per agnitionem Dei morum optimorum corda mundantur. Quid enim profuit Balthasari regi, quod manum scribentem ante oculos suos in pariete conspexit? Cui visioni quia non potuit adiungere mentis aspectum, quaerebat adhuc videre quod viderat. Tali autem acie luminis, qua ista intelleguntur, Daniel praeditus, mente vidit, quod ille viderat corpore. Rursus illa parte animi, quae imagines corporum capit, vidit somnium Nabuchodonosor rex: et quoniam non habebat idoneum oculum mentis ad melius videndum quod viderat, id est, ad intellegendum quod viderat, ideo ad interpretandum visum suum, aspectum quaesivit alienum, eiusdem scilicet Danielis: cui tamen aperienti ut certam accommodaret fidem, etiam ipsum somnium ut sibi diceretur exegit. Daniel autem revelante sancto Dei Spiritu, et quid ille vidisset in somnis ea parte vidit qua corporum capiuntur imagines, et quid significaret mente conspexit. Non est autem propheta veri Dei et summi, qui oblata divinitus visa, vel solo corpore, vel etiam illa parte spiritus videt qua corporum capiuntur imagines, et mente non videt. Sed plerumque in Scripturis sic posita inveniuntur, quemadmodum visa sunt, non etiam quemadmodum intellecta sunt; ut mentis visio, in qua totus fructus est, exercendis lectoribus servaretur. Sed ex multis quae aperte sunt scripta, manifestatur nobis quomodo illa intellexerint, quae sic in libris posuerunt, quomodo figurate illis demonstrata sunt. Ad duo enim genera illa visionis pertinent figuratae demonstrationes: ad mentis autem, id est, ad intellegentiae visionem simplex et propria pertinet revelatio rerum intellectarum atque certarum. Omnia tamen haec genera mirificis et ineffabilibus distributionibus exhibet atque moderatur Spiritus sanctus summae incommutabilisque sapientiae. Sed isti miseri sunt qui calumniantur Prophetae dicenti quod Deum viderit, obicientes apostolicam sententiam, ubi invisibilem dixit. Si enim alter obiciat huic apostolico verbo evangelicum verbum, quo Dominus ait: Beati mundi cordes, quoniam ipsi Deum videbunt; quomodo respondebunt posse invisibilem videri? Verbo enim premunt imperitos, et quatenus invisibilis Deus dictus sit, etsi cognoscunt, cognosci timent. Tanta est pernicies animorum, qui cum vincere hominem volunt, ab errore vincuntur.

The Scriptorium Project is the work of a small group of lay people of various apostolic churches who are interested in the preservation, transmission, and translation of the works of the early and medieval church. Our efforts are to make the works of the church fathers accessible to anyone who might have an interest in Christian antiquities and the theological, philosophical, and moral writings that have become the bedrock of Western Civilization.

To-date, our releases have pulled from the Greek, Syriac, Georgian, Latin, Celtic, Ethiopian, and Coptic traditions of Christianity, and have been pulled from sundry local traditions and languages.

www.ingramcontent.com/pod-product-compliance
Lightning Source LLC
LaVergne TN
LVHW061039070526
838201LV00073B/5105